ROUND THE WORLD IN A WHEELCHAIR

DOREEN WEBSTER

Pen Press

First published in Great Britain by Pen Press

All paper used in the printing of this book has been made from wood
grown in managed, sustainable forests.

ISBN13: 978-1-907172-66-3

Printed and bound in the UK
Pen Press is an imprint of Indepenpress Publishing Limited
25 Eastern Place
Brighton
BN2 1GJ

A catalogue record of this book is available from
the British Library

Cover design by Jacqueline Abromeit

Contents

Chapter 1	Early Days	1
Chapter 2	The Magic of Fiji	10
Chapter 3	Down Under	18
Chapter 4	Bali to Singapore	41
Chapter 5	Cruising the Caribbean	50
Chapter 6	Canadian Cousins	67
Chapter 7	North to Alaska	85
Chapter 8	Dali and Picasso	94
Chapter 9	The Big Apple	99
Chapter 10	Bangkok to Beijing	106
Chapter 11	All About Scooters	143
Chapter 12	Vive la France	147
Chapter 13	A Year of Mixed Fortunes	151
Chapter 14	Sailing Down to Rio	155
Chapter 15	Goodbye Spain	175
Chapter 16	Lessons Learned	180

Chapter 1

Early Days

May bank holiday 1996. It started much like any other day but by the end of it, so many things had changed forever.

We lived in Spain but had returned to England three days before. It was a sunny morning so we decided on a drive round the local countryside. We thought of stopping at the pub for a beer but realised this was England and a bit too early. What a good thing we didn't stop.

Noel got out of the car. It was the last time he would ever drive. He complained that his right foot felt numb. By the time we had climbed up the two flights of stairs to our apartment his whole leg was affected. Within minutes he was losing feeling in his right hand and arm and we realised that he was having a stroke.

As we waited for the ambulance, I watched the side of his face contort and his speech began to blur. It was like watching someone I loved disintegrate before me. My main object became the need to keep him conscious. I felt he must not lose that whatever happened.

The ambulance men carried him down the stairs. He does remember that journey in the ambulance but what happened afterwards at the hospital is a blank. I followed in the car and after they had settled him in the ward, I was told to come back later.

I phoned our family. Not exactly local. Glasgow, Madrid and London. I poured myself a glass of wine, lit a cigarette, and wandered around worrying about Noel in hospital, not really knowing what to do next.

Every July and August I ran a summer school for Spanish and French students. I had returned to England in May to set it all up. I had all the forms to fill in. Perhaps I needed something to concentrate on that would offer some distraction from the awful events of the day. I sat down and did them there and then. When I thought about it afterwards it seemed a strange thing to have done and what surprised me more, I didn't make any mistakes!

Noel stayed in that ward in Worcester hospital for two or three days, while they did tests and saw how things were progressing. The early stage is vital, and fortunately he did not deteriorate any more. They moved him to the geriatric section of the hospital and my heart sank. He was only 68. I knew that ward because my father had spent some time there when he had been ill a couple of years previously. The staff were caring but the general atmosphere was depressing – and that was where they sent my father's teeth to Birmingham with all the laundry, and they were never seen again. My mother had also died in another part of the same building. So it was not a place with happy memories for me. But Noel was getting out of bed and having physiotherapy. I reckoned something good must have been happening. Then the good got better when he was transferred to the special Stroke Unit at Evesham. That was so different. The hospital was quite small with gardens around. The staff were friendly and understanding. Everyone in Noel's section had suffered a stroke but everyone seemed to have been affected differently. As well as paralysis of limbs, some people had lost the ability to speak and to read, others had problems with their sight or their hearing.

But experts were at hand. The two men in the next beds had their names above them – Smith and Jones. I immediately thought of the popular TV programme – Alias Smith and Jones.

Noel had daily physiotherapy and speech therapy. Fortunately his speaking was not seriously affected but he had difficulty formulating his thoughts into words and pronouncing them. His speech has never completely recovered in as much as he cannot project his voice, his pronunciation of some sounds is faulty and he still has to organise his thoughts at times. The physiotherapists had him starting to walk with a stick within a couple of weeks. He was very unsteady but it was a start.

I visited him every day and it was here that I became acquainted with the item that was to feature so prominently in our future life – the wheelchair. I was able to take him into the grounds of the hospital. It was a good summer so we sat outside in the sunshine. His ward also had its own little garden, complete with a pond.

I remember the first time I took him for a walk outside the hospital grounds. The river Avon was just the other side of the road. We went along the towpath and I found myself imagining how I would explain that I had managed to tip him in. He did this himself without my help much later on – but that is another story.

Noel stayed in Evesham until the middle of August. After therapy his speech had improved though the right side of his face was still deformed. He had paralysis down his right side with no use of his arm and hand. He could walk a little using a stick but needed a wheelchair to go anywhere but the shortest distance. As he had only one usable arm, he could not propel himself in one of those wheelchairs with large wheels. I guess if he had done it one-handed he would have gone round in circles!

Now he could go home but not to the home we had before in Worcester.

That was a lovely apartment in what had once been a big country house called The Firs. We had sold our previous house two years earlier because it is easier to go away and leave an apartment for months. Our villa in Spain had been built for us over 20 years earlier as a holiday home. Now we were both retired we lived there for most of the year.

The Firs did not have lifts and we lived on the second floor, up two flights of stairs. Noel had suffered from arthritis for many years and sometimes had problems with his knees. I remember asking him if he would be able to manage the stairs at the time when we considered buying it and he assured me that it was okay. Now it was impossible. We intended to return to Spain as soon as Noel was fit enough but now he was out of hospital we had to find somewhere accessible. We did not want to commit ourselves to anything long term. Our daughter Claire had the idea of looking for a holiday let. It was August so we were in the season. After searching around, we struck lucky. There had been a last-minute cancellation of a small apartment on the ground floor of an old farmhouse at Sedgeberrow just outside Evesham. It was near enough to the hospital for Noel to attend as an outpatient for physiotherapy.

It was ideal for us. The owners fitted a ramp up to the front door and everywhere was flat. The main room had originally been the kitchen of the farmhouse and had a huge range. It had been converted into a very comfortable kitchen-cum-living room. There was also a bedroom and bathroom. As with most bathrooms that have not been specially converted for disabled use, it was no good for Noel but this is something you come to accept. He can only use a walk-in shower. A shower above a bath is no good. But it is possible to wash and keep perfectly clean. Maybe a top-to-toe is not so much fun as a bath or shower but it works. I have become quite a top-to-toe expert for Noel over the years. I remember I was one myself years ago when I was a child. After being bombed out during the war we lived in the bottom half of a house. The people upstairs let us use the bathroom on Friday evenings – otherwise it was the kitchen sink. Houses with multiple bathrooms have made us rather spoilt nowadays.

Fortunately our home in Spain did not need too much alteration to make it suitable for Noel. All the accommodation was on one floor and by adapting the pathway round the back to a ramp we could by-pass the steps at the front. We arranged for this work to be done before we arrived.

By early October we were ready to do our first bit of travelling with a wheelchair.

We had our Spanish car with us in England, so we chose to return on the ferry from Portsmouth to Bilbao. We had travelled on that route before but as two able-bodied people. This would be an interesting new experience.

Our car carried the registered disabled badge. We were directed to a specific lane prior to boarding the vessel and when it was our turn to embark we advanced with warning lights flashing. That tells the men organising the car decks that you must be placed near to a lift.

No problems. There are some disabled cabins and we had one of them, complete with the walk-in shower. Getting round the boat with a wheelchair was easy. The sea was calm. We had a pleasant trip. When we arrived in Bilbao I would have to drive us home – several hundred kilometres.

This was another new experience. I have driven most of my life and had my own car. Indeed we had left that car in England. I had also driven in Spain but like many couples, on the longer trips the man had tended to be the driver or it was shared. There was only one driver now – and that was me. Is that ever strictly true when you have a man in the car, especially one who happens to be your husband? I guess Noel will always tell me how he thinks I should be driving. Thirteen years down the line he is still doing it and it still makes me really mad.

Our trip through Spain was fine. The alterations to our villa were excellent and there we were ready to take up our lives again. We already had a shower and with some slight alterations and the addition of a seat we could both get in together. That's the ideal set-up – friendly and convenient.

We live up a hill and at that time the approach road was very rough, so all trips with Noel would be in the car, wheelchair stacked in the boot. We had lots of friends and a good social life. Things were getting back to normal – albeit a slightly different normal.

Noel could manage to get around indoors with the aid of his stick but could do very little for himself. Having only his left hand would have been easier if that had not been so deformed by arthritis. He cannot bend his fingers and the one he can use points at an angle. He had eight artificial joints in his right hand. It was never really a successful operation and was of no consequence at all now. I worried about leaving him alone in the house at first. There is always the thought that there could be another stroke or the more practical consideration that he might fall over and hit his head on the way. Neither happened.

We went back to England the following May. I still had the summer school in Worcester, which would be host to at least 150 Spanish and French students. Families had to be found for them all, teachers and classroom facilities organised and leisure activities booked for the afternoons. Our flat at The Firs in Worcester had been let and we were fortunate enough to get the same place at the farm in Sedgeberrow, which was about a half hour's drive from Worcester. My car was in the garage at The Firs so we did not need our Spanish one. This time we were going to fly from Alicante to Gatwick. Another new adventure. We had done the journey from Spain to England by plane many times over the years but never with a disabled traveller.

We drove to the airport and left our car in a pound. We soon discovered that air travel presents few problems. Organised help is always at hand. I don't know whether we did so that first time but we quickly discovered that you go straight to the front of the queue to check in. An airport employee escorted us to our departure gate and took Noel in the wheelchair right up to the entrance of the plane. A seat near the front had been allocated and he was able to walk the short distance to it. We took the cushion with us and the wheelchair was put in the hold. At Gatwick the wheelchair came back to the plane and I wheeled him to the luggage reclaim. Only one of our children was in England at that time, our eldest son Andrew, who was then living in Surrey with his family. He met us at the airport. Claire had left Madrid and was travelling round the world for a year with a friend. Roland and his partner, Amy, were on a long stay in South America.

So we were installed in Sedgeberrow again. I was using my English Renault 5 instead of the Clio we had in Spain. We soon realised that for a person whose disability is on their right-hand side, a continental left-hand drive car is much more accessible. Getting into the passenger seat they can lead with their good leg. However, I took him everywhere with me as I supervised the students. He was always a person who enjoyed going out for a drive and was a happy, if sometimes critical, passenger. I did leave him alone one evening while I went to a student disco and I more or less said "just sit there and watch TV" with a urine bottle at the ready. Of course he was perfectly alright.

It is very easy to worry unnecessarily when you are looking after someone all the time and to imagine things that could happen. It never completely goes away but gets less with the passage of time.

I sold my student business at the end of that summer. We also found a buyer for our apartment at The Firs. Time to sort out all our belongings. I made a start with regular runs to local charity shops and a car boot sale at the hospital in Evesham. The staff there were pleased to see Noel again. When we got to the final packing up our younger son, Roland, who is a very strong lad, carried Noel up the two flights of stairs. Once in, he had to stay until he was carried out again.

Returning to Alicante we became acquainted with what I always call the 'forklift'. They rarely have walkways off the planes there and they use a special vehicle for all disabled passengers, which has a platform that can be raised and lowered.

We now knew that travel by plane or ferry presented no problems but we needed a base in England so that we could visit our children and their families. Staying in other people's homes can be very difficult for a disabled person. Bedrooms tend to be upstairs, even worse toilets are often upstairs. Anything but a short stay can cause a lot of inconvenience for everyone.

We decided our area was Sussex. We had lived in Surrey in the past but could not afford it now. Staying at the Travel

Inn in Horsham we started to search and found a one-bedroom ground floor apartment in a village called Partridge Green. We had family in Brighton and near Dorking and this was exactly mid-way between. Problem solved. We moved in just after Christmas.

Now we were able to go back and forth as we wished. A third way of travelling was introduced. I drove through France and took the cross-channel ferry from Cherbourg to Portsmouth. There is a chain of hotels called the Campaniles in France. We found them ideal. They have disabled rooms which you enter from outside on the ground floor. The bathroom facilities are so-so; although the one in Cherbourg had one of the most accessible showers we found anywhere. The Brittany Ferries fast-craft is perfect. We parked our car right by the ramp.

Our experience proved that with a positive attitude much can be achieved. We had both adapted well. I knew that I would always be the one who would have to do everything practical and Noel accepted this. He may be physically disabled but mentally he is alert and interested – and ever ready to offer advice even when it is not required!

He had been a graphic designer and had his own studio before he retired. His hobby was watercolour painting and drawing. He was right-handed but now that side of him was useless. The appearance of a rather unusual rabbit in our garden gave me some ideas for a story I wrote for my grandson. I asked him to illustrate it. With his left hand he found it very difficult but it was a start. Within six months he was painting again and achieving a standard nearly as good as before. Alas, over the years his hand has deteriorated and he can no longer hold the brush.

Mary, a friend of ours in Spain, had owned a travel agents in England that she had handed on to her son. Tommy and Mary were keen bowlers and they were planning a trip with other bowls enthusiasts. They hoped to play matches in various parts of the world.

Noel and I had never had any interest in bowls but we were very interested in the idea of a round the world trip. It was agreed that we should join the group along with another couple who did not play the game. As the plans were drawn up, it became clear that this was going to be the holiday of a lifetime. I was especially excited because, although I had travelled to many countries, I had never been outside Europe. They did not say so at the time, but Tommy and Mary confided to us afterwards that they had been worried about taking along a disabled person in a wheelchair. Perhaps surprisingly, we had no worries. It all sounded fantastic and Noel would do what he could. We had managed everything so far and this was another challenge.

That was how our real travelling started in 1999.

Chapter 2

The Magic of Fiji

We left Heathrow on Sunday 28th February 1999; our group met at the airport. Four of them – Keith, Jenny, Tommy and Mary – were already our friends. By the end of the trip all 25 would be.

At 12.45 we boarded a BA jumbo jet bound for Los Angeles. It was the first time Noel or I had been on a long-haul flight. Add to that Noel's dependence on me and his wheelchair in many unfamiliar surroundings. It was indeed an exciting, perhaps daunting, prospect.

The airline crew looked after us well. Essential number one for anyone disabled on a long flight is easy accessibility to the toilets. That was achieved. Space for two people within them is another thing. Forget about closing the door but otherwise no great problems.

With a window seat we were set for the wonderful experience of the Arctic from above.

The views of Iceland and Greenland were magnificent. It was incredibly clear. The pilot reckoned it was the best he had seen in 20 years. The gods were obviously with us. From over 30,000 ft we gazed in awe at the snowy emptiness of northern Canada.

Right on time, ten hours after leaving Heathrow, we landed at Los Angeles. Help was at hand for Noel and his wheelchair. We were escorted through immigration to collect our luggage.

A guide met the group and we went to the coach. This was to be the first of very many journeys by coach. Something else new for Noel to handle. The steps were far from easy but he managed with my help. We installed ourselves in the front seat and the driver put the wheelchair in the boot. Another hurdle crossed.

It was Sunday afternoon and the freeway was quiet. Even the driver was surprised how quickly we reached our hotel.

The Sheraton, Anaheim is a very large mock-Tudor building. The conference suites all had names like Surrey and Kent. Seemed strange to arrive in the States and be reminded of the Home Counties. We were allocated a disabled room and this was our introduction to the American hotel bedroom. Two absolutely huge king-size beds in acres of space. We always sleep together and always request a double bed but this was something else!

It was late afternoon in LA. Inside us it was well past bedtime. But the rule with crossing time zones is: adapt to your destination. So we had our first meal of the trip – fishcakes with an excellent salad, delicious herb bread and some Californian red wine.

As a smoker in those days, I soon discovered that there was nowhere to light up legally.

The hotel had beautiful gardens where smokers retreated. But what to do with the dog-end? Should I swallow it or bury it in the flowerbeds?

We went to sleep quickly but predictably woke up very early. Our first day and we were off to Disney. That was after breakfast; one of those incredible buffets which are the speciality of big hotels. With so much choice I always wish I had the capacity to try it all.

Buffets do have a downside though for wheelchair users, especially ones like Noel who cannot propel themselves and only have the use of one hand. I have three choices: I can do a tour and report back; I can push him round in the wheelchair first to let him see what is available; I can make the choices for him. Number one requires the sort of memory you need for Kim's game. Number three is not advisable – I would almost certainly make the wrong choices. So it is off for the tour and then back alone to collect the chosen items. With the greater experience of hotels, which we acquired later, you start to realise that most of the buffets are very similar and you know what to choose.

I am not a great fan of Disney and don't like cartoons that much but we were in Anaheim with the theme park just round the corner. Something we really ought to do and were we pleased that we did.

We went with Keith and Jenny, our non-bowling friends, who were helpful to us and were delighted to find that they got the same preferential treatment as Noel. It started with the hotel laying on special transport for us. It continued with no queuing for anything and there were always employees ready to lend a hand. We were beginning to discover that America has a wheelchair-friendly policy with appropriate facilities.

Noel did not go on the biggest roller coasters but we did a splendid boat trip, took the monorail right round the park and walked and walked. I will often refer to 'walking', which actually means me pushing the wheelchair. Fortunately I am an enthusiastic walker.

Perhaps because it was a Monday in February it was not very crowded and we were able to get around very easily. I ended our visit with my doubts dispelled. I was a convert. Nothing was tacky. It was a great fun day out with preferential treatment that could not be faulted.

That evening Tommy and Mary held a get-together in their room; an opportunity for us to really meet the rest of the group. It was the first of many 'cocktail parties'.

We were due to leave Los Angeles the following day but first the morning was put to very good use with a guided coach trip around the city. We started downtown among the big shiny tower blocks and, in contrast, visited the oldest house in the city, which had once been a ranch. There was another stop at Mann's Chinese Theatre in Hollywood Boulevard and a look at the hand and foot prints and writing in the pavement. Then up to Beverley Hills with all its expensive boutiques. We only had time to spend a couple of dollars on a coffee, which was, perhaps, a good thing.

Holiday money was going to have to last for the next six weeks.

The morning had started off sunny but now the smog set in. By the time we reached Santa Monica and Venice Beach we could hardly see the ocean.

But it was time to be in the air again heading for Nadi in Fiji.

Fiji consists of more than 300 islands scattered across 230,000km^2 of the South Pacific Ocean. Nadi is on the largest; Viti Levu and the international airport are situated there.

Another jumbo, this time with Pacific Airlines. It was more than half empty so there was plenty of space for everyone to stretch out during the ten-and-a-half-hour flight. The crew were all Fijian and the food far superior to British Airways.

It was dark when we arrived and raining. A representative of Rosie's Tours met us at the airport. We were all presented with leis made out of shells and boarded the bus with them adorning our necks. Our destination was the Sheraton Royal at Denarau, which is a short distance south of Nadi. It was obvious that it was surrounded by lovely gardens but we would have to wait until the next day to see them. Inside we were greeted with fruit cocktails served by charming Fijian girls in national costume. The whole hotel looked splendid.

Our request for a disabled room resulted in an upgrade and we were taken to one on the ground floor in a completely different part of the building to the rest of the group. We had crossed the date line and lost a day. We were tired after a long trip, and now we wanted to sleep and look forward to what tomorrow would bring.

When I opened the curtains the next morning, I could hardly believe what I saw. Our room was by the most perfect tropical beach: coconut palm trees, soft silvery sand and a sparkling sea. It was deserted apart from a single Fijian fisherman working on his boat. I love the sea; I love swimming. Noel was still in bed but by 7.30 in the morning I was taking my first dip in the warm Pacific water. Absolute magic!

After a sumptuous breakfast we explored the grounds of the hotel. They lived up to all our expectations of the previous night, full of tropical plants, multi coloured flowers and coconut palms. We chatted to one of the local women who made craft items out of local materials to sell to visitors. She told us all about the traditional house she lived in, that she had married at 15 and had 8 children. They make traditional raffia dolls for weddings. She said she would make one for us. We still have it hanging above our bed, the bright coloured raffia long since faded.

Any visitor will quickly learn one Fijian word. Everyone greets you with *bula*, which means welcome. Fijians have ready smiles and are very friendly.

Another swim in the sea, lunch by the pool. About five in the afternoon, the clouds rolled in and the rain started. We were to learn that this was a regular occurrence in this part of the world. December to April is their wet season as well as their summer season.

Walking on hot stones is a traditional Fijian ceremony and we watched a demonstration. Legend has it that the ability to walk on fire was given by a Spirit God to one tribe. In order to perform successfully, firewalkers must observe certain points of preparation, the main ones being two weeks segregated from female company and not eating coconuts. As the ceremony takes place at the Sheraton Royal regularly, I am not sure whether the ones we saw observed these rituals! However, it was very entertaining. We sat in a *bura*, a typical building open at the sides while they performed in the garden.

A very relaxing day. The hotel grounds were delightful and very easy to get round.

An early start the following morning. Another swim before another delicious breakfast and ready for a coach trip by nine o'clock.

Our first stop was the Garden of the Sleeping Giant. Like many islands, Fiji owes its origins to volcanic activity long ago. The mountain, which bears the name Sleeping Giant, is part of the Sabeto range not far from Nadi airport. It is so called because of its shape. Raymond Burr, of American TV fame, founded the garden to house his collection of orchids in the area in 1977. He subsequently sold it to another American who continued development. It covers 50 acres and is landscaped with water features and walks. The collection of orchids is truly fantastic. The terrain was not at all wheelchair friendly but with several people to help, we managed to see sufficient to appreciate the colourful variety of plants and the landscaping. We could have stayed longer but there were other visits to make.

March 5th was International Women's Day and when we arrived in Viseiei, a typical Fijian village that welcomes visitors, we found that many of the women were in their church, which was Methodist, to celebrate. So all the women in our group were privileged to join them for a short time. It seemed really unusual taking part in something which is worldwide in that small village on an island in the middle of the Pacific.

The coach driver took us to Rosie's house. She is the owner of the bus company but was away in Australia. It was on the top of a hill with panoramic views of the surrounding countryside and the bay. A dominant feature is the sugarcane plantations.

Sugar production has been the main economic activity of Fiji since 1883. Once more we were entertained with fresh fruit and juices.

The population of the country is made up of 50 percent indigenous Fijian people, whose original stock was a mixture of Papuans, Polynesians and other Pacific islanders. Of the remainder, 45 per cent are of Indian descent. They first started coming to Fiji in the late 19th century, brought by the British to work on the sugar plantations. Many settled there and they are now a very influential part of Fijian society as they run many of the businesses.

Our last stop was Nadi town. Here the Indian aspect of Fiji was very obvious. They owned most of the shops. Women were wearing traditional Indian saris. There is a large Hindu temple. Time for a bit of shopping. Acme Fashions offered an excellent variety. Although the shop was Indian owned, the clothes had

Fijian origins in their colourful patterns and designs, which would appeal to European/Australasian tourists. We succumbed to a shirt for Noel and a skirt, jacket and tee shirt for me. We still have them all in our wardrobe and we still wear them all – so we must have chosen well.

Back to the hotel for lunch. Noel had been on and off the coach all morning and had survived his many 'manhandlers' well.

True to form it rained again in the afternoon. The bowlers had the first match of their tour scheduled, and as soon as the rain stopped it went ahead. I have no record of whether the winners were English or Fijian but we do remember their comments about the somewhat deadly local brew, which may, or may not, have aided their performance. It is known as *yaqona* or *kava* and is made from the roots of a shrub. Its properties are narcotic rather than alcoholic. Apparently its effect is to give the drinker a slightly numb tongue and throat.

Later in the bar we saw an excellent *Meke*, which is a traditional entertainment of song and dance. The men were in grass skirts and carried spears decorated with feathers and shields. The women wore brightly patterned clothes. It is not done just for tourists but is part of the Fijian way of life. It was all performed with an infectious exuberance and loads of character.

Our third and last day in Fiji again started bright and early. We were off on a boat trip. It was a vessel rather like a ferry between the islands, dropping off and collecting passengers. For us it was a round trip. It was hot and sunny and we sat on the deck, unlike some people who preferred the air-conditioned areas below.

The places we visited had storybook names like Castaway Island and Treasure Island. They had sandy beaches, palm trees and little *bures* (houses made from copra with thatched roofs). We passed mangroves and coral reefs. A group of musicians with guitars played informally on deck. Another bit of Fijian magic.

The weather for the trip had been perfect but after lunch, true to form, down came the heavy rain.

As we had such a superior room with the terrace on to the beach, we were voted hosts for the second 'cocktail party'. Bring your own glasses and drinks and enjoy the sunset. And what a fabulous sunset. I have a photograph. The sky is shaded from bright orange to palest yellow and the palm trees are dark silhouettes. A perfect ending to our stay in a truly lovely place. We had to be up at 3am for our flight to Auckland.

Chapter 3

Down Under

Sure enough, at 3am we received a call and we were airborne by 6am. Don't really want too many of those. We had to be really organised because Noel cannot dress himself. However, this was only a short flight, about two and a half hours. We were picked up by a coach and taken to the Sheraton, Auckland where we were given a really superb disabled room with yet another king-size bed and a very luxurious bathroom.

Noel is an artist. As mentioned before, he was right-handed, but after his stroke, when he became paralysed on his right side, he had become almost equally competent with his left hand. This was despite the fact that arthritis, years prior to his stroke, left his hands very deformed with completely stiff joints. We are both interested in art and wherever we travel, we frequently visit art galleries.

Our first afternoon in New Zealand, we visited the Auckland art gallery. It has an impressive collection of paintings of New Zealand origin, which has been added to over the last century. We enjoyed our tour. However, I have to say that we were equally impressed by the very tasty sweet potato and orange soup they served in their restaurant. I remember saying I hoped it was a sample of the food we were going to receive on our trip.

It absolutely bucketed with rain while we were in the gallery but eased off a bit when we made our way back to the hotel. It was all uphill and I was sweating buckets in my waterproof by the time we got back.

We didn't go out again that evening. Noel watched football on Sky TV in our room. Coventry was playing Charlton. Here we were on the other side of the globe. What a small world it is these days! This was brought home to us even more by receiving a fax during the night from our son in England, just giving us bits of news.

He's a great lad the way he thinks about us.

Not such an early start the next day. This would be an opportunity to explore Auckland. We would be able to wander and find places for ourselves.

Auckland is a big, modern city with lots of high-rise dominated by the Sky Tower which points like a needle into the sky. Water is never far away and the harbour is very impressive.

We went over Auckland harbour on the ferry to Devonport. No problems there with the wheelchair – just wheel on and wheel off.

We crossed back again for lunch with our friends, then we had to take the ferry back to Devonport. Noel has a special cup because he finds ordinary ones too difficult to hold and he had left it in a café on the other side.

The transit bus around Auckland had special disabled access so we took a trip and saw a lot more of the town. New Zealand was already showing signs of being wheelchair friendly, apart from the hills, but being a modern, developed city it had good pavements.

It was only a short stay there but we did manage to cover quite a lot of ground and certainly liked what we saw.

Next morning at eight, we met Dave. He was a Maori who would be our driver for our tour of North Island. We knew that for the next three weeks we would be getting in and out of a coach, sometimes several times a day. Noel and I had evolved a technique, which had worked well so far in the USA and Fiji. Having a driver who knew us should be a great help and Dave turned out to be just that. He was always willing to lend a hand and the wheelchair was always waiting when we left the coach.

Two hundred years ago much of North Island was covered with forests and the giants of the forests were the kauri trees.

Many of them were more than a thousand years old. They grow in two stages. For the first hundred years growth is rapid and they have side branches. After that they shed the side branches and have clean trunks.

In the 1790s they began to be felled for ships' masts and spars, and a thriving business developed. They also secrete an amber resin. This kauri gum became a major export in the latter part of the 19th century. Today there are only remnants of these kauri forests and one of these became our first visit after leaving Auckland.

The museum at Matakohe had features on the history of milling and gumdigging and reproductions of living conditions of the early settlers. There were displays of furniture and carved panels and a collection of beautiful pieces carved from the gum. It was all very well presented. Like all museums, it had a shop and being a collector of natural objects (rocks, sponges, shells, etc), I purchased a piece of kauri gum. It looks just like amber.

A short – and fortunately easy – walk through woodland with many trees and plants which we did not recognise and we arrived at the site of the most enormous kauri tree.

The trunk was huge and bare and soared into the sky. At the top was a vast umbrella of leafy branches. They always say you must put something in photographs to give a true impression of size. Our group below the tree were miniscule.

This was our first experience of the woodlands of New Zealand. There were many treats ahead.

Our destination that night was the Beachcomber Hotel at Paihia, which is on the Bay of Islands well north of Auckland where we had started our journey that day. It was a modern building overlooking the beach and the sea. The facilities were excellent. From then on in New Zealand we would be moving hotels most days but we were staying two nights there.

The following day a boat trip round the Bay of Islands was scheduled. When we got up it was very dull and raining, but the Maori gods were on our side, or perhaps Mary's prayers were answered, and by the time we reached the jetty the sun was coming though. Once more there was no difficulty getting Noel on the boat. The Bay of Islands is a lovely setting and some of the islands are steeped in history. Russell is the oldest town in New Zealand and was the headquarters of the South Pacific whaling fleet back in the 1830s. Captain Cook landed at Roberton Island and Assassination Cove got its name from a massacre and cannibalisation in 1772. Nowadays it is best known for nature reserves. It got quite choppy as we went out to Cape Brett lighthouse and through the 'hole in the rock' but soon calmed as we came back.

Later in the day we visited Waitangi, the place where the Maoris signed away New Zealand to the British in 1840. The museum was very interesting and I loved the Maori meeting house. It was filled with wonderful carvings and there was a strangely peaceful atmosphere. Outside was an enormous war canoe, 35m long that carried 80 warriors. It was carved from three massive kauri trees, like the ones we had seen the previous day. Apparently, it is launched each year for a ceremonial commemoration of the signing of the Treaty. The whole area was surrounded by beautiful gardens, not all easily accessible by wheelchair.

The Beachcomber Hotel, true to its name, was right by a long beach. I am a beachcomber so I went off to collect rocks and shells. Beaches are generally a no-go area for wheelchair users but Noel does not share my love of them, so he is quite happy to stay behind while I go off and wander.

It was the 70th birthday of one of our group, Peter, so that was a good excuse for a party round the pool that evening.

We had a long coach trip the next day, down to Rotorua, so it was on the road by 7.30. There was one visit scheduled on the way – the glow-worm grotto at Waitomo.

This was one occasion when Noel stayed on the coach; wheelchairs and caves do not mix. He didn't miss that much. The grotto consists of large limestone caves, much like any others apart from the glow-worms. A small boat with a guide takes visitors through. I remember that guide because she must have called us 'folks' a hundred times. It is a very common expression in New Zealand.

Rotorua is situated in one of the main geothermal areas of the world renowned for its hot springs, geysers, bubbling mud pools and rising steam. These are evident even in the town itself. It developed as a spa centre at the beginning of the 20th century when visitors from all over the world visited the famous Old Bathhouse. Our hotel, the Lake Plaza, was enormous with its own hot spa pools.

After a good night's sleep in another well-appointed room, a busy morning was ahead. At the Agrodome, there was a great fun show featuring all the different types of sheep found in New Zealand. The special stage was rather like a pyramid where all the sheep were assembled. There was a sheep-shearing demonstration and a mock auction and I managed to get involved as a volunteer to go on stage and bottle-feed a lamb. Outside the sheep dogs showed us how efficient they are at rounding up the sheep. Our memento of the place is what I describe as a 'tickling stick'. It is white, silky soft and far too nice to use for dusting, which I suspect is its real purpose. Then on to the Rainbow Springs on the southwestern shore of Lake Rotorua, so called because of the number of rainbow trout that live there.

At the Whekarewarewa Reserve we went on a train trip around the thermal area. There was boiling mud and steam coming out of the ground all over the place. Well worth seeing but on that day certainly not as dramatic as the guidebooks lead you to believe.

Getting on and off a coach can be tiring for anyone disabled, so it was nice to have the afternoon free to wander. We went to the park and the museum. There was a dramatic audio-visual presentation of the volcanic eruption of Tarawera Mountain in 1886. The seat I sat on actually rocked! Rotorua is an easy, pleasant town to walk around with lovely parks and open areas.

In the evening it was back to Whekarewarewa for a Maori show. The walk through the woods was far from easy but achieved. The show is intended for tourists and hundreds of them attend. However, the singing and the traditional dancing in very colourful costumes was lively and entertaining. There was a meal in a large hut for 250 people. Like most mass catering, it was not brilliant food. But it was a good evening and one of those things you do in Rotorua.

We really didn't feel much like getting up at 6 o'clock but we had to be on the road for 7.30. It was bit foggy at first but that soon cleared when the sun broke through.

Our destination was Napier. Now that is an unusual place. There was an earthquake in 1931, which destroyed all the town. It was all rebuilt in art-deco style. The buildings are ornate and colourful. Noel and I both found it fascinating. We had a guide who was a very enthusiastic volunteer and gave us all lots of interesting background information.

Before going to our hotel, the Travel Inn, Napier, we went to the Mission Estate Winery. We lived in Spain and we drink wine. When we are in England, we often buy New World wines, so we were looking forward to trying some at a New Zealand vineyard. We had a tasting of several but I have to admit that none of them grabbed us that much. We were also going to discover that although New Zealand and Australia are big wine producers, it is not cheap in either country.

Off for my beach walk in the evening, but in Napier it was grey stones and big waves. The beach was redeemed by the beautiful gardens between it and the road.

Dinner at the hotel featured some more of that lovely pumpkin soup. The food in New Zealand was proving to be very good. There was a definite touch of nouvelle cuisine in the presentation but the quantities were generous.

Not such an early start for our trip to Wellington, broken only by a visit to the Mount Bruce nature conservancy for birds. It was not possible for Noel and I to walk all round but we saw a very good film about the wildlife of New Zealand from pre-historic times and how the introduction of predators from other countries had resulted in the decimation of the native populations. Now they are trying to conserve the few remaining members of many bird species.

When we arrived in Wellington it was raining. The coach driver took us on a trip round the city so we got a good overview. We stayed at the Copthorne Plimmer Tower, which had very good facilities. Unfortunately, it continued to rain very hard all evening, so we had no opportunity to explore the city on foot.

Sunday 14th March was Mothers Day in England and I was delighted to find two envelopes under our door with greetings from two of our children. Another plus for the modern world of faxes and computers.

It was goodbye to North Island and to Dave, who had been such a kind and helpful driver. We crossed over on the ferry from Picton. The weather was still poor when we started the crossing but the sun came through and we were able to enjoy some lovely scenery. At the other side we met Des, our South Island coach driver, who was a wonderful character. He had been a driver for many years but was sort-of officially retired and only did some trips that he chose. I don't know why he chose us, but we were very glad he did. He really knew South Island right down to who lived in which house. We felt he might have even have known the names of the sheep!

But I am moving ahead. Our first trip with Des was from Picton to Nelson by a lovely scenic route. Our hotel was called Trailways Motor Inn, another pleasant hotel with excellent food. The level of cuisine everywhere continually impressed us. Des said the river by our hotel was the Nile, but when we went for a walk around, I saw a Maori name, *Maitai*, on a sign. However, Nelson, the town, did seem to have something of a fixation with Nelson, the man, and references to his battles featured prominently in the names of the streets and in Trafalgar Park.

After we left Nelson the next morning, we drove through thickly wooded hills and deep valleys, along the Buller Gorge until we reached the west coast. It was a beautiful road past big beaches where there was virtually no development. At lunchtime we stopped by the pancake rocks. With my interest in geology, I found these absolutely fascinating. They are layer on layer on thin strata of limestone, all completely horizontal. There are blowholes in them and when the sea is rough it shoots up through the holes. Unfortunately, it was a very calm day so the blowhole experience had to be from postcards. This was one of the few occasions so far on our trip when there was no way Noel could get down near the shore. For a wheelchair user natural landscapes of this sort are always going to present the most problems.

We carried on to Greymouth, where we spent the night at the Quality Kings hotel on the banks of the Grey River. Not all the hotels can offer special disabled facilities but so far the bedrooms had all been more than adequate, though some of the bathrooms presented difficulties. Showering was not always possible but washing will always keep anyone clean.

Greenstone, rather like jade, is a feature of this area and Greymouth had several shops selling jewellery and carved objects. We settled for a pair of earrings and a miniature kiwi.

The next day, gold was our object. We were off to Shantytown for a spot of gold panning. We took a short ride on a steam train, our second experience of a little tourist-type train (the first one was in Rotorua) and no problems. Everyone had to sift through gravel in a special pan to obtain a minute amount of gold, which was given to us in a little phial. One-handed Noel could not manage that so one of the experts did it for him. He then spent his time telling me that I was doing it all wrong! However, we both ended up with the same smidgen of gold.

The gold rush in New Zealand began in 1865. At first it was panned from rivers before mining began in earnest. Shantytown is a recreation of an early gold mining township. It is near the site of an old gold claim and it features a blacksmith, fire station, hospital, printing works and a working sawmill. The steam train follows the original sawmill track of the 1800s.

I was very interested in the collection of precious and semi-precious gemstones from the area with the emphasis on Westland greenstone.

Then came one of the highlights of the trip – the Franz Josef glacier. It was pouring with rain when we arrived and we were all kitted out with waterproofs. But the gods were on our side again and out came the sun. We pushed Noel to a place where he could see the glacier and then left him there while we carried on with a guide across a very large moraine to the foot of the glacier, a distance of about a kilometre. It was magnificent, a wonderful shade of blue. Some pieces broke off with a big crash while we were there. All down the sides of the valley were waterfalls tumbling down the rocks. There are longer walks organised which go up on the glacier. That would have been a great experience but just walking up to the face of it was fantastic.

When we returned to where we had left Noel, we discovered that another member of our group had wheeled him back to the coach. There is always someone willing to lend a hand.

On the drive to Queenstown the following day, we really began to appreciate the scenery of New Zealand. It is a small country but there is so much diversity in a short distance. We saw the Fox glacier, the Southern Alps and some incredible blue lakes, which were so still that all the scenery was completely mirrored in them.

Many of the mountains are forested right up to the peaks, others were capped with snow.

Our stay in Queenstown was at the Copthorne Lakefront Hotel. It was very large and it was the first time on our trip that we were disappointed in the food and the service.

However, it was walking distance from the town centre and we had a travel-free day. We were able to explore at our own pace. We wandered round the shops and art galleries and down by the waterside where there were traditional horse-drawn carriages offering rides around the town. There are mountains all around which makes Queenstown a very attractive setting.

It is well known for active sports such as bungee jumping, jet boating, etc, but we did not partake of these! It was the second match of our tour for the bowlers so we went into the park to watch. All the parks in New Zealand are very well kept and this was no exception.

The next morning was also free before we set off for Te Anau. Our only stop on the way was a bird sanctuary. It was very hilly and grassy – neither condition conducive to wheelchair pushing – so we opted out of that one and just sat enjoying the views across the countryside and the nice weather.

The hotel at Te Anau was the first one where we encountered a problem. Our room was on the ground floor but the restaurant was upstairs and there was no lift. So we opted to eat on our own down in the bar. It proved an entertaining choice. There was a big rugby match on TV and rugby has the sort of following in New Zealand that soccer has in the UK. The bar was full of enthusiastic fans watching the match.

Destination the next day was Milford Sound, a distance of about 120km from Te Anau. It was a very interesting drive through the Fjordland National Park, which included the one-mile-long Homer tunnel cut out of solid granite. The mountains in this part of the country are really dramatic. There are sheer rock faces with trees clinging to them and rain forests full of beech trees, giant ferns, mosses and lichens.

Beech are the most common trees in New Zealand and here there were four varieties: red, black, white and silver.

Four hundred inches of rain falls on Milford Sound in a year and as we got nearer, it was obvious that some of it was going to descend that day. It gradually got mistier as we approached. We went for a boat trip. Visibility was very poor and the tops of the mountains were invisible. But we did see many spectacular waterfalls and our search for seals was rewarded by seeing three of them sitting on a rock by the waterside.

On the drive back to Te Anau we stopped at Cascade Creek. This was another highlight of the trip that Noel could not share with me. I had fallen in love with the temperate rainforests and this was the opportunity to go for a walk in one. The variety of plants is difficult to describe. There are so many different types of ferns and ground plants under the trees and the perpetual moistness has resulted in a covering of lichens in yellows, reds and white on trees and stones. It was one of the few occasions on the trip when I was completely on my own, able to appreciate the beauty and tranquillity of my surroundings.

We had another night in Te Anau. It is a favourite place for walkers and there are lots of trails in the area. I decided that if I ever came back I would love the opportunity to explore this lovely countryside on foot.

Time to move on, this time heading for Dunedin, but en route we stopped at Timbertop, a farm run by Bruce and Natalie Pearson. Like so many other New Zealanders, they specialise in sheep, but deer were also an important part of their business. He told us that one of us would have to shear a sheep and our names would all be put in a draw. It was Margaret's birthday, so for a joke the only name in the hat was hers. But she only had to hold the sheep and I also seized the opportunity to hug one again – it was rather bare as it had just had its wool removed.

They sold a range of products made from deer antler velvet. This is removed humanely from the animals under anaesthetic and is known as velveting. When it has been removed from the antlers, it is kept below freezing and taken to a special processor. It has long been an ingredient of Chinese medicine and is reckoned to have many properties for treating arthritis, anaemia, high blood pressure and stress, as well as promoting good general health and healing. We did buy some tablets, which I have to confess neither of us ever took, as well as some pure lanolin from the sheep.

The visit was an interesting and unusual experience. Dunedin has strong Scottish connections and it had the same grey granite appearance of some towns in Scotland. We arrived about lunchtime and after eating, Noel and I visited the local art gallery but were not unduly impressed. We stayed at Cargills hotel, close to the city centre but surrounded by a beautiful garden. There was also a very pleasant courtyard where we sat having drinks before dinner.

Olveston House was built in the 19th century by a Bristolian and it remained in the family until the 1960s. We were thinking this sounds like the sort of stately home owned by the National Trust in the UK and were not that enthusiastic. However, it was pouring with rain, so it was a good option and it proved to be far more interesting than we had anticipated. As with most properties of this type, there is no upstairs access for people with disabilities. However, Noel went round the downstairs with me and they gave him a video about the upper part. In a separate building on the site there was an excellent collection of very well preserved vintage cars.

The building of the Otago Central Railway commenced in 1877. It was not completed entirely until 1921. It played a central role in the transport of livestock and produce in the Dunedin area until its closure in 1990. At that time the mayor of Dunedin announced that the City Council would purchase the section through the Taieri Gorge. which was 60km long. The money was duly raised that year and it became New Zealand's longest private railway.

It was still raining that afternoon when we embarked for our trip on the Taieri Gorge railway. Unlike our two previous train rides, this one had typical train carriages. We started at Dunedin railway station and travelled the 53km up to Pukerangi.

Wingatui at the beginning of the trip is only 34m above sea level, whereas Pukerangi is 250m. The route goes over several viaducts above the gorge giving dramatic views. Like so many of these railways in different parts of the world that go though difficult terrain, you wonder how they managed to build them when they relied on just manpower and not machinery. Our journey lasted four and a half hours and went up to Pukerangi and back again to Dunedin. The weather was dull and rainy but it was still possible to appreciate the scenery. The Wingatui viaduct is 47m above a watercourse called the Mullocky Stream and is 197m long. Both looking along it and looking down from the train were pretty impressive. There was a second viaduct called Deep Stream and well as several tunnels. Here and there were old huts, which had been used by the construction workers.

Early the next morning it was on the road again. Our main destination was Mount Cook. Our driver diverted a little in order to introduce us to the Waitaki valley where all the reservoirs and hydroelectric power stations are situated. They supply the whole of South Island and much of North Island as well. The lakes are vast and very deep and that morning in spite of its being cloudy they were still a brilliant jewel shade of blue.

After lunch at the hotel where we would be spending the night, we headed for Mount Cook. It is renowned for being covered in cloud but the gods were on our side again. As we approached, the clouds gradually moved away and we were treated to a view of snow-capped peaks. A short walk in the area was scheduled, due to last about an hour. Obviously this was an activity not at all suited to wheelchair users. Some of our group decided to take an aeroplane flight over the area so Noel went to the airfield with them and waited there for me. The walk was not as exciting as I had hoped. We strolled around Mount Cook village, but our guide did give us a lot of information about the geology of New Zealand.

The countryside was really stunning. The white peaks of the mountains gleamed in the sunshine. The lower parts of the mountains were a greyish brown. The grass in the valleys was a rich golden yellow. The area between Mount Cook and Omarama is naturally dry with huge sheep and deer stations. That year New Zealand had a drought so it was even more noticeable.

We spent that night at the Heritage Gateway hotel at Omarama. Omarama is a Maori word that means 'The place of light'. Apparently, their warriors and their families used to go there to spend the long hot summers gathering food and relaxing by the

Ahuriri River. The Mackenzie basin is still an area renowned for outdoor recreation, offering fishing, skiing, hiking and hunting.

Thursday 25th March, the last day of our New Zealand tour when we would be heading for our final destination, Christchurch. The weather was superb and we were treated to more views of Mount Cook and Mount Tasman. The countryside was so beautiful in the early morning sunlight, emphasising all the colours of the water and the landscape. There were a few very early signs of the leaves changing colour for the autumn, as there were lots of deciduous trees there, very different from the rain forests further south.

After lunch at a town called Geraldine, we crossed the Canterbury Plains – which are as flat as a pancake and home to millions of sheep – to arrive in Christchurch, hometown of our driver Des, who took us on a tour of the city. He was very proud of his garden and he drove us round to his home so that we could see it and meet his wife.

He had been a lovely, friendly informative guide. We could not have wished for anyone better and we were all sorry to say goodbye.

We checked into the Copthorne hotel where a nice surprise awaited us in the form of a fax from our daughter Claire with all the family news.

Next day really felt like a day off. No coach to get on and off. Nobody to tell us where to go or what to see. This was a day for Noel and I to do whatever we wanted. This was a day of exploring on foot – or my feet anyway!

We started off at the museum and art gallery. It was an excellent museum with displays about New Zealand history and transport and a replica street of old shops. The art gallery had a few interesting paintings but nothing very outstanding. We had a coffee in the main square, bought a good book about the country in the post office and a wooden egg made out of yew in the arts centre. (As well as rocks I also collect eggs and have quite a collection from around the world made of wood, alabaster, etc.)

Sticky Fingers, a café with a terrace on Oxford Terrace, provided us with an excellent salad lunch.

After a wander round the shops we went into the botanical gardens. Christchurch is a lovely relaxed city with Oxford connections. Our eldest son, Andrew, went to Christchurch College in Oxford so we felt a certain affinity with it.

We still had a bit more time there the next morning and we spent most of it in the Saturday craft market where we bought a wooden jewellery box for Claire and a hanging crystal decoration for ourselves. Crystals are supposed to be lucky, aren't they, and we had certainly been lucky having what had been a fabulous tour of a very lovely country.

Many people say that New Zealand is like England used to be back in the 1950s. I can't really go along with that though I can see what they mean. The pace of life is certainly slower than in the UK today and the traffic levels are low. The atmosphere of the cities is safe and unthreatening. The total population is small, there are far more sheep than people, and there is plenty of space for everyone. The standard of living is high.

We had thoroughly enjoyed our stay. I shall always remember those wonderful temperate rain forests. I would love to go back again to do some trekking – though given my role as a carer, that seems a bit unlikely.

But then it was time to move on. Australia here we come.

That afternoon we flew from Christchurch to Brisbane. Once more the airline staff, both in the air and on the ground, could not have been more helpful to us and it was a pleasant, uneventful flight. Brisbane was only a stopover. Less than an hour in the airport, when I managed to lose and find a gold earring, and we were on our way to Cairns.

We all checked in to the Matson Plaza. Much of Queensland is covered with rainforests – not the temperate sort we had seen and loved in New Zealand but the tropical variety. The hotel had lush gardens with many palm trees and a very inviting and interestingly shaped swimming pool. It did not take me long to sample it.

The Matson Plaza is near to the centre of Cairns but we did not venture out that evening.

Sunday morning and it was off to the rainforest. We were going to see it in a variety of ways in several forms of transport. The Cairns-Kuranda railway was first proposed in 1882 when the tin miners of Heberton agitated for a better route to the coast to replace the impossibly boggy road from Port Douglas. Work on building it commenced on 10th May 1886. It started at sea level and finished at an altitude of 327m. The first section to Redlynch had 15 tunnels, 93 curves and dozens of bridges above ravines and waterfalls. All the work was done by hand. The rainforest conditions were bad for the workers and many became sick. There were navvy's camps set up all along the line and it is reckoned that at one stage 1,500 (mainly Irish and Italian) labourers were involved. They were poorly paid and as was common with railway building projects in the latter part of the 19th century, there were many accidents and deaths.

The route now exists for people wishing to visit Kuranda and the train is pulled by a steam engine. We travelled on it that morning. I have a lovely photograph of Noel, triumphantly waving his walking stick, sitting on the train. It was a great journey.

Apart from the scenery of forest, rocks and waterfalls, it made one realise the magnitude of the task of building it without any modern machinery and how the labourers must have suffered.

We spent about two and a half hours in Kuranda, which does have quite a lot of facilities for tourists but nevertheless was interesting. We explored the market and visited a butterfly sanctuary. Being in a tropical area there were some wonderful specimens flying around.

Having arrived on land, we left Kuranda in the air by Skyrail. At a total length of 7.5km it is the longest gondola cableway in the world. In 1999 when we were there it had only been open for less than four years. There are 114 gondolas and each carries six people. Ours carried two people – one in a wheelchair. It was slowed down specially to give us more time to enter and we had it all to ourselves.

The cableway goes right over the rainforest canopy. Having viewed it from ground level on the way up it was a great experience to see it from above on the way down.

The journey commences at Kuranda and there are two intermediate stations Barron Falls and Red Peak on the way down to Smithfield Station, about 14km north of Cairns. Passengers can disembark at these stations if they wish. We got out at Red Peak where there was a short boardwalk to enable people to experience walking surrounded by a great diversity of trees, palms and other plants. It was possible to push Noel on the boardwalk before we were assisted into another gondola for two. As well as passing over forest, there is a section between Kuranda and Barron Falls where the gondolas pass over the Barron River. The cable spans 388m between towers on either side of the river. Altogether a great experience. A great day out and another example of how if you want to do something people will always help you to achieve it.

That evening six of us went out into Cairns in the evening. There are lots of bars and restaurants there. We had a good meal. Bugs were on the menu – but we did not try them and I still do not know what they were. But things could only get better. The next day was the Barrier Reef. We went by coach to Port Douglas and then boarded a Quicksilver catamaran. No problems at all with access to the catamaran. It was quite a large boat. Our destination was a pontoon on the reef. There were three reef viewing possibilities – diving, snorkelling or taking a trip on a submersible. I opted for the first. I had never dived but our youngest son is keen on the sport and he had dived on the Barrier Reef as well as lots of other parts of the world. It was my ambition to do it too. So I signed up.

I was allocated to the 1.30pm group and given a form, which, if I recall rightly, gave me some responsibility for the results of my actions. Some rudimentary instruction followed. We had lunch on the boat. Obviously there was only one viewing option possible for Noel, if we could get him on the submersible. The crew were great. His wheelchair was left behind and they carried him down the steps and into a seat. I went with him. There were myriad shoals of fish all around us and wonderful views of the coral. Noel decided that having got down there he might as well go for a second trip. I left him to get ready for my dive. They got him on the boat and presumably if they didn't want him as a permanent fixture they would get him off again.

In the warm waters of the reef it is not necessary to wear a wetsuit for a short dive, so I soon emerged in my bikini, staggering under the weight of the equipment. It really is very heavy out of the water. I spotted Noel back in his wheelchair watching from the side.

I was in a group of six people with an instructor. Two of them changed their minds and did not go. The rest of us went down, trying to get accustomed to the underwater breathing technique. It is strange at first but once I felt confident I really enjoyed it. There were several large blue fish which came up to us and we could touch them. There were corals of all sizes and shapes and loads of small multi-coloured fish.

I had purchased an underwater disposable camera and the instructor took photographs of me. Not that you would probably recognise me easily with the goggles and everything! We stayed down for about 30 minutes. By then I was feeling relaxed about it all and would have liked to stay longer. I felt really pleased with myself that I had done it and I have the PADI certificate as a souvenir of the experience.

It was back to the hotel where we all had a party in Andy and Margaret's room.

Noel and I went down to Cairns on our own the following morning for a quick exploration of the town before our departure after lunch. We visited the local art gallery where there were many examples of aboriginal art. Most of it was upstairs and we thought it might be inaccessible. But they had a very large lift at the back of the building used for taking works of art etc up to the galleries and that day it came in useful for two people and a wheelchair.

Our son Andrew likes all sorts of music and plays a number of instruments. We decided to purchase a didgeridoo for him. No way were we going to add that to our luggage so we mailed it from the post office.

When we got back to the hotel there was just time for a quick beer and sandwich before we set off to the airport. It was an extremely humid day. We had been lucky to have such a lovely sunny day for our trip to the reef.

We flew from Cairns to Sydney – an uneventful internal flight. We passed through so many airports on our trip that it was all becoming quite routine. There was always help available should we need it.

It was dark and very much cooler when we reached Sydney. We were not unduly impressed by the Millennium Plaza. It had no special disabled facilities but it was modern and high-rise so access to the rooms was no problem. After a meal in a cheap café nearby, Noel and I decided to take a walk though the local streets. It quickly became apparent that we were in the red light district of the city. There were plenty of sex shops and strip clubs. It might have been amusing to have taken Noel in his wheelchair into some of the clubs but they all had steps down to them and it had been quite a long day so we settled for meeting up with the rest of the group for a coffee in the café opposite the hotel before retiring to bed.

We had a few days in Sydney, so there was ample opportunity to do some exploring of our own. We took a taxi down to Darling Harbour for a boat trip. The weather was dull but Sydney Harbour would be impressive in any conditions. We got a splendid view of the opera house and the bridge. It is possible to go high on the structure of the bridge and there were several people up there as we passed. I must admit that would have been a very inspiring experience.

The aquarium close to the harbour was certainly well worth a visit. There are tunnels under the water and as you walk through there are sharks, stingrays and innumerable other types of fish swimming around you . Different sections are devoted to various habitats. We have visited other aquariums since then but it certainly rates as the best.

Time for lunch. If you eat fish in Sydney it will probably be snapper – so for us it was snapper and chips. And it was here that I was introduced to cinnamon on the top of my cappuccino. Much nicer than chocolate – I always ask for it now with variable results. Several restaurants have raided their kitchen stock cupboards on my behalf.

Usually overground and underground railways are impossible for disabled people to access but to our joy the Sydney monorail presented no problems. It can be used to reach most of the major attractions in the city and provides a bird's eye view. We took a trip all round and then disembarked at the city centre. We went round the main shopping plazas and then walked all the way back to the hotel. It was uphill much of the way but I was getting into my 'walk around the city' mode.

It is worth mentioning at this point that taxis are obviously a good choice of transport in cities. Most taxi drivers are usually helpful, though sometimes less so than other categories of people, and there is usually room for a wheelchair in the boot. Later on I may mention one place where this was not necessarily true.

Thursday 1st April – perhaps it did turn out to be a bit of an all fools day in one respect. A coach trip to the Blue Mountains was scheduled and we set off in pouring rain and heavy mist. We stopped briefly at an animal park. In Australia you must see the koalas and the kangaroos and I duly photographed them to show to the grandchildren. But it was such a commercial place – the shop was larger than the animal pens!

We drove on through the gloom to an IMEX cinema way up in the hills. We saw a film called 'The Edge' all about the Blue

Mountains area. It was a very good film, which is just as well because we were not going to see the real thing that day.

This was followed by a barbecue lunch in the cinema, which sounds a bit bizarre in itself. But the Cajan chicken was good.

Our driver decided that we might as well forego the scenic railway as we were not going to see any scenery. This was 1999 and Sydney was due to host the Olympics in 2000 so we went to the Olympic stadium instead. It was very impressive and they were way ahead of plans. As we now know, the Olympic games there were very successful. So that was a plus in an outing which could have been disappointing.

The following day would be Good Friday so that evening we phoned our daughter, at work at lunchtime, to wish all the family a happy Easter in Scotland. She had been in Spain the previous day. We are not the only ones who keep travelling around!

After a dinner in the hotel, we went to bed hoping for better weather the next day so that we could continue our exploration of Sydney.

But it was still raining hard and being Good Friday almost everything seemed to be closed. However, the Contemporary Art Museum was open so we took a cab there. We are not great lovers of Andy Warhol, who was their special feature at the time, but we both loved the exhibition of Aboriginal crafts, especially some beautiful weaving done with natural fibres, feathers and seeds. Noel paints landscapes himself and is not a great lover of some types of modern art but we were both very taken with the colours and textures of aboriginal painting. Earth colours – browns, yellows, greens and ochres – tend to predominate. Intricate patterns of lines, dots and other motifs are used along with representations of animals, birds and fish. We purchased a book by Howard Morphy who is Professor of Social Anthropology at University College, London, which contains a great selection of illustrations and background material.

At the Visitors' Information Centre, we watched a video on the history of the city. We had a drink at a bar on the Rocks and then a really excellent lunch at The Rock Café, obviously a very popular venue and deservedly so. It was really humming with people. Very near the Rock Café was the Billich Gallery at 100 George Street. We had never heard of Charles Billich, perhaps surprising because his work has been exhibited all over the world in places as far apart as Abu Dhabi, Tokyo and Rome to name a few.

He is an Australian and among his many achievements he was appointed official artist to the Australian team at the 1996 Atlanta Olympic Games. Many of the pictures in the exhibition we visited had a sporting theme but there were also cityscapes of Sydney, New York and Tokyo and some lovely silkscreen prints. We were very impressed and really enjoyed his work. It had been very much our sort of day in spite of the rain.

That evening we went for a short local walk with the object of buying a bag. The only luggage we had at the start of our trip was one case and a small backpack, but we were collecting all sorts of souvenirs along the way and our capacity had run out. We stowed everything away before going to bed as we would be leaving the following day.

However, our visit to Sydney was not quite over. Straight after breakfast we took a cab to the Opera House. It has a million steps up to it, a bit like a Mayan temple, and it looked very inaccessible. However we were told that if we went back at 11.30 we could be part of a special trip for disabled people which uses many lifts that other trips don't.

To fill in the time we took a little train round the botanical gardens nearby, full of lovely flowers and trees.

There was only the two of us and a couple of Americans on the disabled trip round the Opera House, and we had a very informative guide. Maybe we did not see everything but certainly enough to make us realise what an absolutely spectacular building it is. It was designed by a Danish architect and after our tour we went to the Custom House and saw a video about its construction as well as models of the whole city and the Olympic site.

At 2.45 we left for the airport. We both agreed that Sydney had been a very rewarding experience and perhaps a place to visit again some time – though with a big wide world out there, I don't really believe in going back. There is too much else to see.

Chapter 4

Bali to Singapore

Now we were bound for Bali. The flight was five and a half hours but with a book to read and a film, it went very quickly. When we arrived in Denpasar it was raining heavily.

Our hotel, the Santika Beach, was in Kuta, which is a popular resort in Bali. Our room was situated at ground level and all the rooms in that part of the hotel were around a swimming pool. The hotel had beautiful gardens full of tropical plants. Sunday April 4th was a day of leisure with plenty of time to appreciate our delightful surroundings. The weather was very humid but also nice and sunny. We took a stroll down the road outside, which was teeming with life. There were lots of local shops and stalls. It was possible to approach the beach directly from the hotel.

The following day was a very busy one, visiting lots of places via a coach trip. Our first destination was a performance of a Barong dance in a local town. It took place in a small outdoor arena and was very well attended. The Barong is a play that portrays an eternal fight between good and evil spirits. The barong is a mythical animal, which represents the good spirit, and the Rangda, a mythical monster, represents the evil one. The story is complicated. It involves actors playing the parts of animals such as the tiger and the monkey, as well as masked dancers. Many humans are involved, a witch and the god Siwa. At one stage the Rangda tries to kill and eat Sadewa, one the main characters, but the Rangda himself gets killed and goes to heaven. In the last act there is a lot of changing from one animal to another, from a boar to a bird for instance, and of course, in the end good triumphs over evil and the Barong wins. The costumes were very creative and colourful and the action very dramatic. Without necessarily following the plot completely, it was nevertheless highly entertaining. As a one-time primary teacher, I couldn't help thinking it would have been marvellous for children who would really have appreciated its imaginative nature.

Our second destination was a village that specialised in woodcarving. Many of them were wonderfully intricate. We purchased a panel to hang on the wall. It has three layers of carving featuring birds and plants. The amount of detail is incredible.

The central area of Bali is volcanic and it was there we headed for lunch. The Kintumani restaurant is high up on the Batur Mountain. To quote their promotion leaflet – "Gentle clouds pass by as you settle down to enjoy one of the most delightful luncheons you will ever remember". There were certainly some clouds around and our guide suggested that if we wanted to take photographs we did so before lunch as the weather might change. And he was right! There was a very dramatic storm and the rain came down in sheets. The view completely vanished. The Kintumani was a very large restaurant. The food was varied and the decorations on the buffet tables very dramatic. It was obviously a popular tourist destination and was very busy.

The rain continued after lunch and to the embarrassment of the guide and the trainee who was with him, the coach leaked. It provided us with quite a bit of amusement as people put umbrellas up inside the vehicle and it subsequently got us a five-dollar discount. (US dollars were a very popular currency in Bali at the time as the local rupea was worth so little. There were 8,000 of them to the dollar and over 12,000 to the pound sterling. I don't know whether this is still the case.)

Bali is 87% Hindu. Our guide, a Hindu, told us quite a lot about their beliefs before we arrived at a temple. It was all in the open air and really seemed rather tatty, especially as it was still raining. Noel gave this one a miss. Apart from the weather the whole site was hilly with lots of steps. I was not unduly impressed at the time but strangely it looks very good in my photographs with lots of beautifully colourful carving and decoration. We noticed on our way back to Kuta that most of the houses have their own small temples and shrines and we saw many women with plates or baskets of offerings for the gods. They leave these on the pavements and all over the place.

Our last call of the day was an art gallery. It was reasonably accessible for the wheelchair but Noel found the paintings and carvings a bit disappointing, though they were housed in a rather nice building. What we really found charming there were lines of ducks walking through the surrounding rice fields.

That was a touristy day but despite the rain an interesting and enjoyable one. It was great to see the Balinese countryside with all the rice fields.

Tuesday started with the swimming pool outside our veranda going green. For some reason it was a really bright shade and quite unusable. Never mind, there was always another one, which was where I had my morning swim. However, the hotel decided that in view of this pool problem we and others should move rooms. In retrospect, I am not sure why this was necessary but we went along with it.

It was another relaxing day – pizza lunch on the terrace, a visit to the laundromat and purchasing beer for a party in the evening organised by Keith, Jenny, Barbara and Mercia. We were all taking turns to host parties during the trip. The venue was to be a raised Bali-style pavilion in the grounds of the hotel. It had a roof but open sides and when the rains came down, as seemed to be a feature of Bali later in the day, we eventually all had to paddle to a nearby restaurant. The room-moving fiasco ended when we returned to our original one at 10pm.

Wednesday was another relaxing day, lazing round the pool (but not ours, which was still a more delicate shade of green) eating and drinking. There was a visit to the bank to obtain a few thousand rupeas for a spot of shopping. Kite flying was a favourite pursuit and there were many original designs for sale on the beach. I reckoned our grandsons would like these.

Just down the road from the Santika Beach hotel was the Kartika Plaza, a really enormous establishment. We all went there for dinner and to see the Balinese dance show. Balinese dancing is fascinating, especially the hand movements, which are such an integral part of it. The dancers wore close-fitting silk dresses in vibrant shades of yellow and red with elaborate gold headdresses.

Next morning we awoke to a blue pool. Whatever caused the green had gone. Time to take advantage of a swim. Noel does not swim – there is no way he could get into a pool – and fortunately for him, he does not share my love of it.

Our last morning in Bali. Massage is very much a feature of the place. You can have one on the beach. However, I decided to try one in the hotel. It was the first time I had ever had a massage and I imagined a gentle, relaxing experience. Not a bit of it.

I had quite a pummelling for what may have been an hour and certainly seemed like that long. The comment I put in my diary at the time was 'interesting'!

Just time for a last bit of shopping. Down to the shops by the beach where I bought three tie-dyed dresses – a full length, a knee length and a mini.

In the afternoon it was time to get ready for the flight to Singapore, the last destination on our world trip. Bali had been very relaxing and now we were heading for a city again.

As usual, everything at the airport was very straightforward with Noel getting all the customary assistance. The flight was only two hours and there was no time difference. We ate on the plane and went straight to bed when we arrived.

Our hotel was the New Otani. It is on the bank of the Singapore River next to Clarke Quay. It is large with 408 rooms and all the restaurants, bars and facilities you would expect.

At 9am the next morning we had to be ready for what they call an orientation trip by coach around the city. The idea is to give you a quick overview of the place.

Stop number one was a Hindu temple, which was just on the edge of China Town. Noel stayed in the coach for this one. These sort of trips can be tiring for anyone with disabilities, as they involve getting in and out rather a lot. This was followed by a half-hour walk around China Town itself. We then went up to the highest point in the city where there was a great view of the harbour etc. It is possible to cross over to the other side by cable railway but there was no opportunity to do that just then.

The gem factory also proved to be inaccessible as the showrooms were upstairs, so I did that one on my own. There were some very interesting pictures made out of small pieces of stones in brilliant colours. A large example with peacocks and flowers was magnificent. We purchased a smaller one to give to Tommy and Mary as a little thankyou present for all their splendid organisation on the trip.

The National Orchid Garden was more accessible with its array of hundreds of different blooms. It houses 700 different species and 2,100 hybrids and is reckoned to be the largest display of orchids in the world.

Our last brief stop was Little India and we resolved straight away that we would return there on our own during the next few days.

That ended the organised bit of the day – quite a lot of visits in one morning.

Left to ourselves in the afternoon we went to the Singapore Art Museum.

There was an exhibition called 'Monet to Moore' sponsored by the American Sara Lee Corporation. It featured many paintings by European artists (impressionist, cubist, etc). Noel was surprised that he had not seen most of them before. As well as this visiting exhibition, there was also a good collection of works by Southeast Asian artists.

On the Singapore river are small craft known as bum boats. They were originally used to transport goods and immigrants from the large boats at the port. Nowadays they are pleasure boats taking people for trips down the river. They started from the quay near our hotel. It was early evening and with the lights on it was an appealing idea. Could we get Noel on? There were several steps to be negotiated. But he is not one to be daunted; neither does he mind being carried in his wheelchair. Three Chinese lads took him up on the boat and we went down river past all the modern high-rise buildings to the statue of the big white lion. When we got back, they duly carried him off again. I have a photograph in which he does look just a little apprehensive. What you cannot see is our faces as we watched and wondered if he would end up in the river himself!

We finished off a very eventful day with an excellent Thai curry sitting on the quay. It was a lovely warm evening. Our friends went back to the hotel but we took a stroll around the market stalls and bars before retiring for the night. We felt we had certainly seen a lot of Singapore in a single day and there was more to come.

The next day was Saturday. The bowlers had a match scheduled, which did not involve us so we were free to wander wherever we chose. We started off by taking a cab back to Little India. Singapore is a very clean, very orderly place. There is almost something sanitised about it and we liked Little India because it was a bit scruffier and it smelled of spices. Somehow there was more character. We were also on a mission to buy a carved dish, which we had seen on our first brief visit. The bowl rests on a very intricate stand, which is carved out of one piece of wood, and it is impossible to see how they did it. Gold jewellery is also a feature of this part of the city and one street seemed to consist solely of shops selling Indian jewellery.

Indian gold has a beautiful bright sheen and Noel treated me to a pair of carved hoop earrings. We had an incredibly sweet coffee, which was served in a beer tankard in a little café on the corner before taking a cab to Suntec City, a huge modern shopping centre. These are the really easy places for wheelchair users wherever you are in the world. Singapore is very warm and they certainly had the air conditioning in the centre at full blast – and if there is one thing we do not really like it is air-conditioning. Most of the time I would rather be hot!

To keep the retail experience going we headed for Orchard Street, the main shopping area of Singapore. Being Saturday it was very crowded and we enjoyed soaking up the atmosphere. Our only actual purchase was lunch in a French deli.

We ate out again on the quay in the evening and then finished off the day listening to music in a Caribbean bar. The world is a truly international place.

Raffles Hotel is synonymous with Singapore. This was the last day of our world trip so what could be more fitting than all celebrating together with tiffin at Raffles.

And before eating, it had to be a Singapore Sling. Apparently, this special drink was created at the beginning of the 20th century by a Chinese bartender, Ngiam Tong Boon. It was originally intended as a drink for ladies, hence the bright pink colour, but nowadays it is assumed to have a universal appeal. It contains gin, cherry brandy, pineapple juice, Cointreau, Benedictine, grenadine and a dash of angostura bitters and should be topped with a garnish of pineapple and cherry.

We have a photograph of our daughter, Claire, when she was on a round the world trip, sitting in Raffles. She is wearing a long Indonesian-style dress and holding a Singapore Sling. I was wearing the dress I had bought in Bali and was determined to have a similar photograph. I have to confess she looked more glamorous than me – but never mind, I achieved the ambition.

Our group were given a room to ourselves just off the main restaurant with lovely views of the courtyard through the windows. The food was buffet-style and what an extraordinary selection of items. There were sandwiches, pies, Chinese-style dumplings, scones with jam and cream and loads of cakes and desserts. We all tucked in. The restaurant was called the Tiffin Room and what we ate was referred to as 'high tea' on the receipt. All frightfully English apart from the odd Chinese items!

Raffles has been subjected to a considerable amount of restoration in recent years. Everywhere was very beautiful but one got the feeling that probably some of the original atmosphere had been lost. Like most establishments these days, there was a commercial aspect in the shape of shops. But we were all really pleased to have been there and enjoyed a pleasant, sociable afternoon.

Now the end really was in sight. It was back to the hotel then off to the huge and modern Changi airport. Noel and I were taken by a different route to everyone else from check-in to the boarding area. It was very devious and went through lots of back areas that passengers do not normally see.

The flight from Singapore to London takes 13 hours. It was very smooth, there was plenty of legroom and we slept much of the way. We arrived at Heathrow at 5.15am to be met by our elder son Andrew.

What a wonderful trip it had been. We had seen and experienced so much in very good company. Tommy and Mary had been a bit worried at the outset about how Noel would cope, but their doubts had proved to be unfounded and they were as delighted as we were that everything had gone so well. He had missed out on very few activities, coped admirably with getting around, especially on and off coaches, and had derived so much pleasure and satisfaction from the trip.

Now our appetites were whetted. For the moment our travelling would be confined to going between England and Spain – but not for long.

Chapter 5

Cruising the Caribbean

Later that year we started thinking about where we would like to go next and began to explore the possibility of a cruise. Although it was not very long ago, cruising was not widely advertised. There were few articles in the press and no promotion on TV.

We knew virtually nothing about cruising. We did not think in terms of which ship or which cruise line to select. Our interest was in the itinerary and there was one in the Caribbean, which appealed, mainly because it visited mainland South America as well as several islands and went into the Panama Canal. The ship was the *Emerald*, the company was Thomsons and the price was reasonable. So we booked up for the following spring.

All cruise ships have a few disabled cabins. They called them cabins then – now they are referred to as staterooms! Ours on the *Emerald* was located close to the main lifts. It had twin beds but our cabin steward soon put them together.

The *Emerald* was quite an old vessel, and we now know after experience on much newer ships that it was not completely convenient for a disabled passenger, but with its wonderfully helpful crew that really did not matter. In fact, we were not aware of it.

So on Tuesday 21st March 2000 at 11.30am we were on board a Boeing 767 of Britannia airlines bound for Santa Domingo. We had two seats together by a window, and the eight-and-a-half-hour flight went quickly. There was a four-hour difference, so it was still afternoon when we arrived.

To our delight, there were virtually no immigration formalities. We did not have to reclaim our luggage, which was taken direct to the ship, and we had transit by coach from Santo Domingo airport to the *Emerald*.

Our enthusiastic local guide on the coach gave us a potted history of the Dominican Republic en route. Our impression was that everywhere was a bit run-down, but I was impressed by something that I was going to notice again when travelling to other parts of the less developed world. There were lots of children about in school uniforms, and they all looked so clean and immaculate.

The ship had no facilities for a wheelchair user to go aboard by the usual entrance, so Noel and I went in via the kitchens on the lowest level of the ship. This became the regular routine for entry and exits, and with the more than willing assistance of the kitchen staff, this presented no problem. It was sometimes necessary to make way for food supplies coming in and rubbish going out!

We had a light evening meal, watched a show, were introduced to the cruise reps and retired to bed about 10pm, which felt more like the middle of the night.

The following day was at sea. After breakfast, we went to a presentation about all the trips which were on offer at our various ports of call. We realised that some would be quite unsuitable for a wheelchair user. We chose five and discussed whether they would present any problems and decided that the other days we would go independently.

The day passed pleasantly, mostly up on the Lido deck as it was glorious weather.

Many ships these days have systems where passengers can choose when and where they eat. The *Emerald* had the traditional first and second sittings for dinner, always sitting at the same table with the same people. We had opted for the second sitting at 8pm. We were allocated places close to the entrance. There were six of us – two other disabled people and their partners. They were all pleasant people and it worked out okay.

The officers on the *Emerald* were Greek and that evening we would all meet the captain, Markellos Kotrozos. It was an occasion for formal dress. He shook hands with everyone – the first of many photo opportunities. They certainly try to sell you photographs on cruise ships.

The staff were very multi-national, many of them Filipino or Eastern European. Our cabin steward was Bulgarian, and the waiters at our table Rumanian. Without exception, everyone was charming and helpful, holding doors open for us and generally offering any assistance they felt was needed.

Our first port was Montego Bay in Jamaica, the second largest city on the island, after Kingston. It features many colonial-style buildings. Another historic property is Rose Hall. The mistress of this great house was reputed to have murdered her various husbands and lovers when she got tired of them and sexually abused her slaves. She was commonly known as the White Witch. Like many grand residences in various parts of the world of that era, it was furnished rather similarly to some National Trust properties. We discovered that we had not been that well advised because there were loads of steps, which made most of it impossible for Noel. I had a quick look around while he stayed outside and we both had a drink of Witches Brew, which was well laced with rum.

The gardens were lovely. We were struck by the similarity of vegetation to the part of Spain where we live – there were lots of bougainvillea, oleanders and castor oil plants. There was a man doing some woodcarving and we bought a snapper fish.

Montego Bay is a rich resort. There were lots of expensive houses and holiday hotel complexes like Sandals. There was also MacDonald's, KFC and Burger King. Is it impossible to get away from them these days?

We had a shopping stop when Noel added another baseball cap to his collection, the first of many on the trip. Like so many markets the world over, there were lots of stalls selling exactly the same rather touristy things and some very garish clothes.

The vendors were all lively and friendly. They were eager to sell but quite willing to accept no as an answer with a smile.

We returned to the ship with the feeling that we had only had a rather superficial view of Jamaica but we sailed on at five in the evening.

Our next port was Puerto Limon in Costa Rica, which was a much more interesting location.

Costa Rica is a very small country, only 51,000km², but it has an incredible variety of flora and fauna. There are 850-odd species of birds and countless varieties of butterflies. Commercially, they are big banana growers and export 2.8 million bunches of them through Puerto Limon annually. There are many national parks and wildlife reserves and it was regarded as one of the world's first destinations for eco-tourism.

Puerto Limon has a population of 75,000, many of them from Jamaica, China and Europe.

We had chosen to go on a trip of the Tortuguero canals. The boat was small and open but Noel was carried on quite successfully. The guide, Enya, was very well informed about wildlife. We saw lots of birds – egrets, kingfishers, herons and vultures. The banks on either side were covered in dense jungle with occasional clearings.

We saw glimpses of howler, white-face and spider monkeys but they moved very quickly in the trees. The Indian Brahmin cows were easier to photograph as they kept still. Crocodiles were basking by the banks.

The first part of the trip was on a river. In some places the water was completely covered with water hyacinth. Apparently, it was originally an African plant and had become something of a pest in Costa Rica. The boat felt as if it was passing through a dense jungle of low plants on the water. From the river we went out into the estuary before heading back into a narrow canal, part of the network of canals that is all over the country.

Going back, we drove through banana plantations and were amazed to see that the bunches on the plants were all encased in blue plastic bags. We were to see the same thing in other places in the Caribbean. It is obviously to protect them but it does look rather strange.

On the bus everyone was telling the guide what animals they had spotted on our canal trip, when what should come down the road but llamas and elephants. The circus had come to Puerto Limon.

The port was only a few minutes from the town centre so we were then able to do a bit of exploring ourselves. We strolled round the market. Another cap was added to the collection.

Back on the ship, we spent another pleasant evening. The catering was excellent. We now know that this is true of all cruise ships. It would be quite possible to stuff oneself all day, starting with a breakfast buffet, followed by lunch, afternoon tea, dinner and for those with the appetite and the stamina, late-night buffets as well.

We are not enormous eaters and I am proud to say that we did not put on weight on our trips. But some people can certainly put away vast quantities of food – it is as if being available, it must be eaten!

We were due to reach the approaches of the Panama Canal at 7am the next morning and to be through the locks by about 8.35. So it was up early for this great experience. However, the schedule turned out to be much later and we did not actually go through until 10.30.

The Spaniards had dreamed of finding an easy crossing of the isthmus between the Atlantic and Pacific oceans. Indeed Charles V of Spain ordered the first survey of a proposed canal as early as 1534. But for more than three centuries they made do with donkey treks and later a narrow gauge railway. In 1880 Ferdinand de Lesseps, builder of the Suez canal, started work, but disease and financial problems defeated the French. In 1903, Panama signed a treaty with the USA who took over the construction. It took ten years to complete construction at a cost of 387 million dollars – a vast sum of money in those days. Among their other problems they had to actually dig through the Continental Divide, the mountain backbone of the Americas. It opened officially on August 15th 1914, cutting the journey from one ocean to the other by 3,000 miles.

We started our trip into the Panama Canal waiting by the port town of Cristobal where pilots boarded our ship. There were an amazing number of vessels of all sizes queuing to go through the locks into the canal.

We went through Gatun locks, where ships are raised or lowered 85ft in a continuous flight of three steps. Each lock chamber is 110ft wide and 1,000ft long. Cables are attached to the ship from special 'locomotives' to guide it straight in the lock. There was a tremendous quantity of water going in and out with the change of levels. It was a fascinating experience.

On the other side of the locks is Lake Gatun. We were surprised at its size and were told that it covers an area of 163 square miles, the largest manmade lake in the world. It was formed by the largest earth dam in the world at that time. There were more queues of vessels on that side waiting to pass through the locks. However, the scenery around Lake Gatun was lovely with forests and hills in the distance. We spent about two hours in the lake before making the return trip back through the lock, when we watched a small boat take our pilot off again. It was certainly something not to be missed and quite impossible to imagine without seeing it.

The Lido deck of the *Emerald* had been specially decorated with branches of palm trees and this was where we spent the time enjoying our trip into the Panama Canal. A special barbecue was arranged for lunchtime. It was a hot day but there was a good breeze.

The next day the ship docked at Cartagena de los Indios in Colombia. We had decided to do our own thing there and took a taxi to the city centre. Our driver, Jorge, thought we wanted a taxi tour but my Spanish was good enough to assure him that was not what we required. We planned to explore on foot – and wheelchair.

Cartagena was founded in 1533 and was one of the busiest ports in the New World as the Spaniards took all the gold and silver out of South America back to Europe. It was also a great haven for pirates of all nations including Francis Drake. Walls were erected around the town for protection, which are still there today. It is a very picturesque town with many lovely old buildings. The whole impression is various shades of terracotta and golden yellow.

I have a poor sense of direction but Noel impressed me with the way he seemed to know how to get round to the places we wanted to visit. There were some fascinating craft shops in the arches, which used to be the old prison. Unfortunately, the cathedral was closed but we went in the church of Santa Marta.

It was not an easy place for a wheelchair – and that is a bit of an understatement. The kerbs were high, the pavements very uneven, but we managed. There were street vendors everywhere. Their current speciality seemed to be t-shirts. When parties of tourists appeared they really sprung into action. But we were on our own. People on our ship complained afterwards that they had been pestered all the time. We were never hassled. These same traders were the people who were only too ready to give us assistance if we needed it.

Colombia is famous for emeralds. We had arranged with our taxi driver that he would meet us at a certain time outside a specific jeweller's shop. The owner of the shop persuaded us to come in and view her stock. At the equivalent of £800 for a pair of earrings, there was no chance that we would be customers.

We loved Cartagena city centre. It was very vibrant and Spanish. However, our driver took us back via Bocagrande, the modern resort area of the city, and it was much like others all over the world – high-rise and fast food outlets.

When we got back to the ship, the sniffer dogs were waiting. With Colombia's drug reputation they were obviously taking no chances.

The next day was also spent in Colombia at Santa Marta. Having read *The General in his Labyrinth* by Gabriel Garcia Marquez, I knew something of the history of Simon Bolivar, who liberated much of this part of South America from the Spaniards.

He is obviously much revered as we had seen monuments to him in Cartagena and I knew that he died at Santa Marta. The Quinta de San Pedro Alejandro is a memorial to him.

We took a taxi again, but this time kept it for a tour. Our first visit was to the Quinta de San Pedro Alejandro which is a national monument. There were many Colombians visiting the site, which has beautiful parkland around it with some fabulous old trees. We were fortunate to have a guide to ourselves who spoke English.

One of the old apartments is preserved as the room where Simon Bolivar actually died.

Our driver Oscar suggested that we should go to Tayrona, which is a small beach resort. It was only a short drive and gave us an insight into how the ordinary people lived, which was mostly in one-storey shacks. There were many of them sitting outside on their verandahs. The beach was rather disappointing but it was obviously quite a popular place as there were stalls, shops and restaurants.

Back at the city centre, we said goodbye to Oscar and set off to explore on foot.

It was an exceedingly busy place with far more traffic than Cartagena. There were masses of people everywhere. It was late on a Tuesday morning and there were groups standing around and talking all over the place. Thinking of all the people we had seen sitting on their verandahs earlier on, we did wonder whether everyone was laid back or unemployed.

It was a difficult town for a wheelchair partly because of the state of the pavements, but also because many of the streets had market stalls and pavement vendors.

However, again, everyone was very helpful and considerate.

We had thought we might be able to get some nice souvenir in the markets but the prevalent goods seemed to be sports socks and imitation Nike trainers. Unlike Cartagena, which obviously catered for tourists, Santa Marta was much more a city for the local population.

When travelling from one part of the Caribbean to another, it is normally simplest to use US dollars rather than obtaining the local currencies. However, when we had a beer in a small hotel in the town, it was a great performance getting change.

We both agreed that we had enjoyed our visit to Colombia very much. It had a real buzz about it and being able to speak Spanish was a definite advantage. We also realised that choosing to go it alone had its advantages. Many of the organised trips were quite short and one could end up back at the ship long before sailing time. If you only have a day to experience a place, you want as many hours as possible. We also felt that we had triumphed over adverse conditions in terms of wheelchair friendliness and our knowledge that there are lots of people out there who are only too willing to lend a hand (and lift a wheelchair) had been further strengthened. Even policemen will get involved.

Our next destination was so very different. Aruba was ignored by the Spaniards because the only crop it seemed to have was cactus. It was colonised by the Dutch who developed ranching to supply beef to the trading ships and the slave markets of neighbouring Curacao. When the slave trade was abolished, the ranching foundered and their only export was the gel of the aloe vera cactus. In the 1830s gold was discovered. Three million pounds of it was extracted. When the supply was exhausted, they went back to aloe vera. Then oil was discovered in Venezuela and Aruba had oil refineries until the boom collapsed. The aloe vera cacti are still there in great quantities, but Aruba now relies on tourism and welcomes thousands of visitors every year.

As we approached the island Oranjestad, the capital came into view. Its architecture is very elaborate and colourful and, frankly, reminded me of something out of Disney.

We had signed up for a trip round the island and a very good choice it turned out to be. It is a strange place – very arid with little vegetation except the ubiquitous cacti.

Our first stop was an area that had been used for gold mining. There were no habitations there but the coastline was very dramatic, far removed from the sandy beaches near Oranjestad beloved by the tourists. There were huge black volcanic rocks with the waves pounding them. There are clusters of boulders all over the island. We went to the Natural Bridge, a rock formation where the sea comes underneath and you can walk over the top or look up at it from the beach below.

The rock in this area was coral. There is a superstition that if you put stones in little piles it will bring you luck. Visitors do this – so there are little piles all over the place. Needless to say, we did the same. I went and explored the beach area while Noel stayed up at the top near the coach.

We were told that there are goats on the island but it was a very hot day, so I reckon they had all found some shade somewhere. The only wildlife we saw was one donkey and a lizard.

It had been planned that we would visit St Anne's church but there was a funeral taking place so that had to be abandoned. We drove back through the main tourist area with its American hotels and timeshare properties. This is where Aruba makes its money and is no doubt responsible for unemployment being only five percent.

Now we had time to look at Oranjestad in more detail. The main street Wilhelminastraat (no doubt named after the Queen of the Netherlands) typified the local architecture. There were loads of designer boutiques, which obviously catered for their rich American visitors. Everywhere was spotlessly clean, everyone was very well dressed, and everything seemed highly organised. Nobody hassled you to buy anything and it was so easy to get around that we did not need help. It was an example of Dutch efficiency – so different to the Spanish chaos of the previous day. Somehow it rather lacked character and reality.

It is interesting that no foodstuffs are grown on the island. Venezuela is only 15 miles away and fresh produce is imported from there by boat.

That evening there was a party on the Lido deck and we did not sail until midnight. It was only a short distance to our next destination, Curacao, which had also been a Dutch colony.

Curacao was one of the main trading centres of the Caribbean. Consequently, when slaving was abolished in the 1860s, it was left in a state of depression. When oil was discovered in Venezuela in the early 20th century, it benefited in the same way as Aruba, and when the slump came it also suffered. Tourism has become supremely important for the island.

Willemstad, the capital, is very colourful. The houses along the shore were painted in many pastel shades topped with red roofs. The two parts of the town are divided by a canal and connected by the Queen Emma pontoon bridge, a slender pedestrian walkway crossing the harbour, which opens to allow large vessels to enter. We went into town by ferry because the bridge was open but were able to walk back over it.

This was one occasion when the choice of activity was for me. I was going snorkelling, something that Noel would not be involved in except as a spectator.

We left Willemstad in a boat called *Waterworld*, which he was able to board without too much difficulty for a half-hour trip to Curacao beach. Apparently the island has 38 beaches altogether and we passed a few en route. I had about an hour's snorkelling, which was great. The water was wonderfully clear and there were shoals of brightly coloured fish. I particularly like some electric-blue ones, which were nearly transparent, and about 9-in long. In addition, there was also a sunken wreck in the area to swim around. Noel stayed on the deck of the boat and took photographs of me. He used to be a semi-professional photographer and a member of the Royal Photographic Society and it had been a great disappointment to him when he no longer had two hands to hold a camera. We had devised a system whereby the camera was attached to his wheelchair by a flexible lead, rather like the sort you get on reading lamps, and he was able to take photographs – though seldom to his satisfaction. Regrettably, with the deterioration of his left and only usable hand, due to arthritis, he can no longer operate it. But that day he took many shots of me in the water and told me that my bum was sticking up! I really enjoyed the snorkelling experience.

We went back to Willemstadt and spent the rest of our time exploring the town.

Like Oranjestad on Aruba, it was very clean and orderly with many good shops. We preferred the architecture. An interesting feature of the town is the Mikve Israel synagogue, which was built in 1732, and the oldest one in the western hemisphere. It is a lovely old building and we were able to go inside.

Like most cruise ships, the *Emerald* had lots of activities to entertain the passengers. I said at the outset that we chose the trip for the places we would visit. However, we did get involved in some of the things available. We often went to the shows in the evening, which were generally of quite a high standard. There were often games of various types on the deck and that particular evening I participated in something called 'This is Your Life'. I can't actually remember what was involved but I must have been successful at something as I am the proud possessor of a giant-sized Thomson's pencil! There were quizzes, darts tournaments, bingo, deck quoits, etc, but we are not really great games players. We had chosen cruising for the places to visit and fortunately on this one there was a new destination every day.

We were scheduled to visit Caracas, Venezuela the next day but due to a landslide this was not possible. Plans were changed so that we could go to Isla Margarita, which is just offshore. We docked at the port of El Guamanche on the south of the island where the scenery was very barren and were taken by coach to the town of Porlamar about 35 minutes away. It was something of a shopping mecca. I am not sure, perhaps it was duty-free. There were certainly plenty of shops selling all sorts of things that we were not interested in buying. The pavements were rather impossible and did not seem worth the effort. All we spent was two dollars on two cans of beer, and they only had non-alcoholic. There were several other trips arranged as well as ours to beaches etc, but nobody seemed to have enjoyed Margarita very much. It was the first time that Thomsons had ever called there – and Noel said he hoped it would be the last!

Our remaining destinations were all part of the British West Indies, and having experienced Spanish and Dutch we were interested to compare.

We were due to dock in Grenada at 9am but were delayed until 11am because another ship was in our place. Grenada is known as the 'spice island'. Nutmeg, cloves, mace, cinnamon and ginger are all grown there. It is very beautiful with lush green rainforests covering all the hills.

This was another occasion when we decided that we would hire a taxi for a tour. Because these islands are reasonably small, it is possible to cover quite a lot of ground in quite a short time, and we were beginning to realise that this was often our best bet.

We started off an Annandale Falls where water cascades 30ft into a pool below. Locals dive off it to get tips from visitors. After that we headed for the Grand Etang nature reserve, which is a bird sanctuary and has a bright blue lake formed from the crater of an extinct volcano. It was a very worthwhile drive. The vegetation everywhere is fantastic and our driver pointed out nutmeg trees and coffee and cocoa plants. He also proudly pointed out the new cricket stadium, which had just been built that year.

St George, the capital, was only a few minutes' walk from where we had docked. It was a charming town with a beautiful harbour. Noel likes traditional boats and was very taken with a four-masted schooner that was moored among many other vessels. There were loads of stalls selling spices. The exotic smells permeated everywhere and we bought a selection to take home with us. I had a nutmeg ice-cream, which was rather unusual and delicious. It rained late afternoon – the first rain since we had started our trip.

We thought Grenada was a very attractive island but as we drove around we did not feel that the people were very happy. Even the children didn't seem to smile much. At the tourist sites they were really after money. Apart from jumping into the water at the falls, they followed you around making up songs about you.

On Sunday 2nd April it was off to St Lucia. Our intention had been initially to walk into town from the ship but being Sunday everywhere was closed, so we decided to do the same as we had in Grenada and go on a taxi tour. And what a good choice that turned out to be.

St Lucia is part of the line of jagged volcanic peaks known as the Windward Islands, which divide the Caribbean from the Atlantic Ocean. It has high mountains and thick rainforests. In the past there were several battles between the English and the French for possession of it. It eventually became British but there is a French legacy in some of the place names. Some locals speak a partly French patois, but the official language is English.

It is indeed a very picturesque island with pointed volcanic hills covered in rainforest to the very peaks. There is a vast variety of vegetation. We saw many very large banana plantations and passed through several villages. There were lots of people and children dressed in their 'Sunday best', and we encountered many minibuses full of local people. Our taxi driver told us it was a 'mothers and fathers trip day' and it was obvious that everyone was out enjoying themselves.

He was very friendly and informative. He showed us lots of the fruits growing on the trees and even picked mandarins and bananas so that we could taste them.

Our destination was a volcano that gives off steam and has hot pools and bubbling mud. It was not high up as we had expected and not as inspiring as we had hoped but it was well worth going for the interesting journey there. We saw the famous twin volcanic peaks known as the Pitons and got a view of Marigot Bay, with its beautiful sandy beach – just one of many on the island. We drove through Castries, the capital, on the way back but did not actually explore in on foot.

The shops in the town were closed, but Pointe Seraphine, a modern complex of duty-free outlets down by the harbour, was open. We had a wander round there and added to the cap and t-shirt collection. It would have been nice to explore the market in the town, which is renowned for its exotic spices, tropical fruits and many variations of the local brew – rum. It is also noted for local crafts, but it was Sunday and we were leaving that evening.

In Grenada we had felt that the local people did not seem very happy. There was a very different atmosphere in St Lucia. Okay it was Sunday and a day off, but we were told that St Lucians do have a reputation for being friendly and chatty and it certainly seemed that way.

Of all the places we had visited on our trip, we liked St Lucia the best and we would have liked to stay longer. Perhaps we may be back there one day.

We arrived at our last destination, Barbados, early the next morning. Barbados is reckoned to be the most successful island in the Caribbean. It has 260,000 inhabitants. The British landed there in 1627 and Barbados is still very obviously British.

We had booked an organised trip, a jeep safari. It turned out to be great fun.

There were six of us in our vehicle and four jeeps altogether. The drivers, young and local, were like a comedy act but they were also very well informed. We did a lot of off the road driving through sugar plantations and forest until we reached the north side of the island. This is not the tourist area. The coast was rocky with lots of rough Atlantic surf. Certainly not a place for swimming. However, between the rocky areas there were smooth sandy beaches and I did manage to get my feet in the water, which was lovely and warm.

Noel stayed in the jeep for the journey because the terrain was not suitable for a wheelchair but he was able to enjoy the wonderful scenery, especially as the sides of the vehicle were open. We also enjoyed sampling the sugar cane, which is delicious, and drinking rum punches.

We returned via the part of Barbados that I suspect most tourists see and enjoy – the hotel complexes and the big houses of the rich alongside lovely sandy beaches.

But as I have said before, all these modern areas tend to look the same wherever they are. They just don't have character.

When we got back to the ship, we discovered that Noel's walking stick had been left in the jeep. Now this was serious. He cannot even stand without it. However the reps contacted the jeep company and we got it back the next morning.

We had the morning free before our flight back in the afternoon. We took a local shuttle bus into Bridgetown, the capital. It is a busy town and we were struck by how British everything seemed to be, right down to their Trafalgar Square with its monument to Nelson – which apparently pre-dates the one in London.

It was a very humid day. We had a walk around, which was not too easy because the pavements had very high kerbs. There were loads of duty-free shops. We made a few small purchases – a polo shirt for Noel, an eye-shield for when I play tennis, some rum cake. Then we made our way back to the ship to get organised for our departure. We had a coach transfer to the airport and waited there because our flight was slightly delayed. Just as we were boarding it rained very heavily, which probably explained why it had been so humid. But we had only had rain twice on the whole trip.

It was an excellent flight back, and we arrived at Gatwick about 7.30 in the morning to a very cold England, which had had snow the day before. Snow on April 4th, but it did not last and we had lovely weather before we were airbound again, this time heading back to Spain.

We both agreed that our cruise of the Caribbean had been a great success. We had chosen the itinerary well and had enjoyed visiting many interesting places. As we realised later when we went on other cruise ships, the *Emerald* was not as convenient for a disabled passenger as some of the newer ones. But we didn't know that at the time and we had no complaints. All the crew had been great, from the captain down to the kitchen hands who had assisted Noel on and off the ship. Everyone had been friendly and helpful. The food had been excellent. We had coped very well with all the trips we had chosen and had discovered that taking a trip in a taxi can be an excellent way of being introduced to places.

Chapter 6

Canadian Cousins

Edgar, Noel's cousin, was born in Belgium. When war started he and his older brother Tony were sent to England. Tony joined the Grenadier Guards and was killed in action in Tobruk. Edgar lived with Noel's family for many years before he emigrated to Canada in the 1950s. They had known each other very well but as he didn't return to the UK they had never met again. Edgar had married a Canadian and they had a son and daughter. We had always kept in touch with the family, mainly through Christmas letters and photographs. Edgar died a few years ago but we continued to correspond with his wife Angie.

We were both interested in the idea of visiting Canada, particularly the Rockies and maybe this slight family link was another incentive.

Thus, it was on Sunday 13th August 2002 we left Heathrow at midday bound for Calgary.

We had considered whether we would do our trip across the Rockies on the Rocky Mountaineer railway or whether we should book a trip where we travelled by coach. We came to the conclusion that the latter would be the more suitable. From our world trip three years previous, we knew that Noel could manage to get on and off a coach with assistance. The difference this time would be travelling with strangers as opposed to a group of friends.

We informed Travelsphere that Noel was a wheelchair user and they agreed to our booking their trip.

The flight with Air Canada took nine hours. Everything went very smoothly. We were now very used to airports and air travel and realised that there are no drawbacks for a disabled passenger. In fact, there are pluses: you don't have to queue to check-in and there is always a special person to escort you to the plane.

When we arrived at Calgary we were met by our guide for the tour and discovered that we were part of a group of about 40 people. Sheila, our guide, turned out to be an absolute gem. Throughout our trip she was determined that Noel would miss out on nothing that could possibly be achieved.

It was three in the afternoon. We transferred to our hotel, the Sandman, a modern multi-storey building right in the centre of the city.

I don't know what we had expected in Calgary but we were surprised. It is very modern, based on a grid system and mostly high-rise in the downtown area.

It is the administrative centre of the oil industry in Canada and many large international companies have their offices there.

It was Sunday so we were seeing the population at leisure. There is a very nice river with walkways. However, a lot of people were not walking – they were jogging, cycling and roller-blading. There were many very proficient exponents of the latter.

It was very easy to push a wheelchair along the path by the river and we made our way down to Eau Claire market with its outside cafes. We sampled our first Canadian beer in one of them. I think the waiter referred to it as a 'grasshopper'. It was very light and refreshing with a slice of lemon.

There was a great children's play area with paddling pools and water sprays, which they could, and did, fire at each other. It was sunny and the whole atmosphere was very pleasant and relaxing. There was an indoor market area. We had a look around and shared a Chinese meal of ginger beef, rice and chow mein from a quick food outlet. Interestingly, it was quite different to the Chinese food we ate in Spain.

Back to the hotel to go to bed. What a long day but we had done what you are supposed to do when you cross time zones, which is try to adapt immediately to their times instead of going off to bed in the middle of the afternoon!! What a nice introduction to Calgary we would have missed if we had done that.

We slept well but woke early. The weather had changed and it was raining. I don't ever recall before watching TV in bed at about six in the morning, but it was a good way to get some local atmosphere.

Like most big hotels, there was a wide choice of food for breakfast and lots of items were much sweeter than I would want at that time in the morning. But we were in the land of maple syrup.

Now we were going to start our coach trip to Banff. It was agreed most amicably that other people would rotate seats but that we should have the front one all the time to make it the shortest distance possible for Noel.

We stopped at Fort Calgary historic park. The site was first developed in 1875 by the North West Mounted Police, who arrived at this junction of the Bow and Elbow rivers to construct a fort. They came with the view of establishing law and order. The fort had a very chequered history being destroyed several times, but more recently archaeologists have rediscovered much of what had been there. The 1975 centennial was when it was designated a national historic site. We were given an interesting talk and video presentation and looked round the museum. They have a 'raising the flag' ceremony every day at the remains of the old fort, but it was belting with rain so Noel and I gave that a miss. Rain and wheelchairs do not go together too well.

The winter Olympics were held in Calgary in 1988. The site is now Canada Olympic Park, which combines a host of recreational facilities with being the training centre for Canada's winter Olympics athletes. One of the Canadian bobsleigh team gave us a talk about the place and showed us a video. After a quick snack in the cafeteria, we joined the Trans Canada Highway heading for Banff.

Banff is a popular tourist town both in summer and in winter, when it becomes a centre for skiing. It is at an elevation of 1371m.

Its earlier claim to fame was the natural hot springs in the area. The heated water does not originate under the ground. It starts as surface water from rain or melting snow, which filters down though cracks in the rock. As it goes down through the earth's crust it gets hotter – one degree for every 33m until at a depth of 3km it would reach boiling point. This hot water becomes pressurised and comes back up through cracks to the surface, forming hot springs. In the 19th century, spas were very popular for the treatment of many ailments. The Canadian Pacific railway was completed in 1884. Construction of the Banff Springs Hotel began two years later and opened on June 1st, 1888. More than 5,000 visitors arrived that first summer. Over the years there have been many changes and additions to the current hotel, the latest in 1990. It can now accommodate 1,700 guests in its 770 rooms. It was one of a chain of prestige hotels belonging to Canadian Pacific but they no longer own it.

When we reached Banff it was still pouring with rain so we drove up to have a look at the outside of the Banff Springs Hotel. It certainly is a most impressive building in lovely surroundings.

Sheila suddenly spotted a female Canadian Mountie in traditional costume, which was quite unusual. She was invited on the coach, and as well as providing a photo opportunity she told us a bit about what she did.

Although it was still raining, it was decided that we would go up Sulphur Mountain which has a cable railway with gondolas. These were enclosed so the rain would not present too great a problem. But just as we approached, the sun came out. The gondolas travel 1560m at a speed of 4m per second up to an elevation of 2281m (7486ft). It was an absolutely brilliant ride over dense forests of conifers. We had a bird's eye view of the Banff Springs Hotel as we went up and the view from the top could only be described as breathtaking with other mountains all around. Noel went into the gondola in his wheelchair, so that was very straightforward.

We checked into our hotel, the Mount Royal in Banff Avenue, the main street of the town. It was a traditional building. They had tablemats showing how it was 90 years ago and the outside had not changed too much, although people no longer arrive in vehicles drawn by horses. Now some of them arrive like us on Brewster's coaches. We were due to spend three nights there. The room was very satisfactory. After we had checked in, we went out to a local restaurant for an excellent steak meal.

There was a trip organised for the next day. Our first visit was to the Takkika Falls, a very impressive waterfall down a mountainside. Below was a lovely white-water river with stands of conifers on its banks. The skies were still cloudy but the air was clear.

Our coach driver was called Bob. Our guide Sheila and he had often worked together on trips and had a very good rapport. They were both able to give us lots of interesting background information and point out things that we may well have otherwise missed.

So it was with the spiral train tunnels. Bob was telling us about them and we were just at the appropriate point on the road when a freight train came along the track. These trains are incredibly long and we were able to see the front emerging from the tunnel while the end was still visible higher up just approaching it. One end was coming out when the other had still not entered and these were not short tunnels. Our timing had been immaculate.

Lunch was scheduled at Lake Louise Lodge, a restaurant at the foot of the Lake Louise, sightseeing gondolas. It was going to be problematic for Noel to get from the restaurant to the foot of the cable railway, but Sheila was not going to let that defeat her. She organised a golf trolley and a driver to get him there.

There is a choice of travelling up the mountain in a closed gondola or an open chair for two people. We opted for the open version. They put Noel's wheelchair on the one before us so we could see it travelling up the mountain as well. It takes 14 minutes to reach an elevation of 2057m (6750ft). The ride was wonderful. As the restaurant area receded, everything was so peaceful, suspended on our own in the open-air way above the slopes below. It was a still, clear day and we could see mountains all around topped by big white clouds. It was possible to alight at the top, which was probably the reason for sending the wheelchair ahead of us, but we decided we would just stay on for the trip down again.

We carried on to Lake Louise itself, named after Princess Louise Caroline Alberta, the fourth daughter of Queen Victoria. The train station nearby dates back to the end of the 19th century and was used until the service was discontinued in 1990. It has been redeveloped as a restaurant and has several restored railway carriages on site. It is a favourite place for train buffs but we did not come into that category.

By the shore of the lake is Chateau Lake Louise, which started life as a log chalet in 1890. It is situated in an area which appeals to mountaineers and walkers and is also popular with artists for its scenic setting. It now has the capacity for 1,000 guests in 515 rooms. It is huge and palatial and the whole area was absolutely teeming with tourists. We walked around the hotel grounds and explored inside. A harpist, Deborah Nyack, was performing in the very grand entrance hall. We listened to her for a while before purchasing a CD.

It is a very impressive building with restaurants and shops inside, all done in very good taste, but, as I remarked to Noel at the time, if I was going to pay the sort of money that I am sure you must to stay there, I really would not want to have a hundred million tourists traipsing around.

Lake Louise is renowned for its blue colour. Apparently, small particles of glacial sediment are suspended in the water. They are very tiny and uniform in size and they reflect the blue and green wavelengths of light. The lake is 90m deep, 2.5km long and 550m wide. Mount Victoria with its glacier is at the end of it.

The whole setting is lovely but one would be able to enjoy it more away from the height of the summer tourist season.

We drove on to Lake Moraine, which is also very blue and is surrounded by ten mountain peaks. It was much quieter than Lake Louise. Noel stayed with the coach but I walked up the trail so that I could view it from above. The water was a deep shade of turquoise.

Another pastime in the Canadian Rockies is seeing what wild animals you can spot. This was a good day. We saw a black bear and a grizzly bear. Apparently, bear sightings are quite rare and seeing both in the same day definitely rated as very lucky. We also saw elk, chipmunks and red squirrel.

A most rewarding day filled with unforgettable experiences and scenery. We returned to the Keg restaurant again that evening to top it off with Mexican fajitas and our usual tipple – red wine.

There were some optional excursions the following day but we chose to spend it on our own exploring Banff. It started life known as Siding 29, a stop on the Canadian Pacific railway. George Stephen, CPR's first president, came from Banffshire in Scotland and the town got its name from his birthplace. Another prominent resident of the town was James Brewster, and his family were influential in the development. In 1904 they had the monopoly of horse-drawn taxi services in the area. You may recall I mentioned that we were on a Brewster's coach. Although they were bought out by Canadian Greyhound in 1965, the name has been retained.

We started our day of exploration with a leisurely breakfast at the hotel, something you don't do too often on organised trips. We had a look around the shops. Some of the retail outlets were a bit touristy but others were very good. As I have mentioned before, I am interested in rocks and fossils and a shop opposite our hotel had the best selection I have seen anywhere. My birthstone is garnet and I purchased a piece of rock with garnet crystals in it.

Banff is situated on the Bow River. There is a paved walkway from the town to Bow Falls, which is wheelchair friendly and very easy to negotiate. We walked part of the way and had a snack lunch in the gardens nearby. It was a very pleasant area.

If there are any art galleries around we are bound to find our way into them. The Whyte Museum had an exhibition of wild flower paintings in the Main Gallery. They were not the delicate watercolours often associated with the subject. The artist Maureen Fair had produced large oil paintings often portraying riotous meadows.

We then visited the Canada House art gallery. This was a commercial enterprise that specialised in promoting the work of Canadian artists. There was a large display of contemporary paintings and sculpture with a special section devoted to native and Inuit work. Each month there was emphasis on one artist. The people there were very friendly and we spent a long time chatting about their exhibits, even though it was obvious that we were not in the market as buyers. In fact, our only purchase was a book about Les Thomas whose work we particularly liked. They were large canvases of animals such as bears and elks in oils, highlighted in a most unusual way with colour and brushwork – and extremely difficult to describe in words!

We gave them our email address so that they could send details of their various exhibitions through to us and they did so for several years. Noel also sent them email versions of his own paintings as a way of saying thank you for some very interesting and inspirational material, all by Canadian artists we had never heard of.

Being a Mason, Noel was interested to see that there was a Masonic Temple in Banff and had it been accessible would no doubt have tried to have a look inside. However, it was up a rather long flight of steps and may well have been closed at the time.

Melissa's was a well-known restaurant on the edge of the town in a traditional house with gardens. We had heard people talk about their excellent breakfasts. So that evening we thought we would try it for dinner and, sure enough, the food was excellent.

Back to the hotel to pack up ready to move on to Jasper tomorrow. We had enjoyed Banff and the area around it.

However, we were not heading straight for Jasper. There were lots of places to take in on the way and we were on the road by 8.30am.

The Icefields Parkway is reckoned to be one of the most scenic routes in the world and we stopped at the information centre at Lake Louise to collect some maps of our trip along it.

It was a beautiful morning, very sunny with a clear blue sky. We stopped at Lake Peyto, another stretch of blue water surrounded by mountains. I was able to wheel Noel along a path from the coach to a point where we could view the lake. We were in for a surprise. A film crew were making a Bollywood film, with a very good-looking Indian lead actor. We gathered that it was something about an alien.

However, this in no way detracted from our enjoyment of the scenery but added another dimension to the experience.

We were scheduled to visit the Athabasca Glacier at 1pm. The Columbia Icefield, with an area of 325km^2, is the largest icefield in the Rockies and the most accessible. Glaciers flow out from it in several directions and the Athabasca is one of them. It is accessed via a very busy centre with special snow coaches, which can drive right out on to the ice, once again carrying the name Brewster. This was where Noel had more than special treatment. They have disabled vehicles to take wheelchair users down to the snow coaches. Not only that, he had a very attractive student named Crystal to look after him. She organised his being lifted complete with wheelchair by a forklift attached to the vehicle and stayed with us all the way to the glacier.

Having arrived, I was able to push him around on the ice in his wheelchair, which was something a bit different. We were on the tongue of the glacier and we could see it stretching above us up the mountain, gleaming a pristine white in the sunshine. As we were about to leave the clouds rolled in and it started to rain. The gods were timing things well again.

After a coffee stop at the Sunwapta Falls Lodge (Sunwapta means turbulent waters), we reached Jasper at about 5pm. Our best wildlife spotting of the day was a black bear feeding beside the roadside. Jasper is quite a small town on the Athabasca River. The railway station is in the centre of the town. We were booked in to the Tonquin Inn for three nights. It was a modern hotel, walking distance from the town centre, with a nice garden. Before dinner I went for a swim, a sauna and a Jacuzzi.

Another full day was ahead of us. We stopped at Pyramid and Patricia Lakes. They were completely calm with beautiful mirror reflections of the surrounding countryside. I have a lovely photograph where the thick forest of conifers, the snow-capped mountain and the clouds above are all reproduced perfectly in the water.

We drove past Medicine Lake, which has many soak holes in the limestone where the water just disappears into underground caverns to emerge much later in the Athabasca River.

We visited the Athabasca Falls where the water tumbles down in a white foaming cascade throwing spray high into the air. I was able to wheel Noel quite close. There were signs warning people not to go to the edge of the rocks and I have a shot of a Japanese man doing just that silhouetted against the water pounding down behind him.

On to Maligne gorge. There was a café and a shop there and Noel stayed in the upper part, the path down into the gorge being impossible. I walked down and over a bridge. The river runs below through coniferous woodland with huge vertical rocks on both sides and foaming white water.

After lunch at the gorge café, we carried on to our main event of the day, which was a boat trip on Maligne Lake, which is the largest one in the Rockies. It is 22km long. The weather was absolutely perfect, and we went on quite a small boat out to Spirit Island, where we were able to disembark. It is a very peaceful setting. Noel just sat and enjoyed the scenery. I walked around, as I usually do, soaking up the atmosphere and looking for photo opportunities.

We drove on back to Jasper and I have to say that Sheila and Bob had once again proved excellent guides with a mine of local information.

That evening we walked into the town and had a meal in a Greek restaurant.

There were optional excursions the following day and this was the one occasion on the trip when I chose for myself. I went white-water rafting on the Athabasca River while Noel remained at the hotel. Again the weather was perfect and the scenery absolutely stunning. The trip was much less hairy than I had anticipated having listened to our younger son's stories of a similar activity in various parts of the world, but it was great fun. We all wore our life jackets and got tossed around on the water.

Afternoon was for relaxing before an evening trip up to Miette hot springs. They are the hottest ones in the Rockies with an average temperature of 53.9 degrees centigrade. Apparently, in 1910 there were plans to develop the area with a spa hotel but Charles Melville Hays, who was about to instigate it, was on the *Titanic* when it sunk and the scheme died with him.

The springs are approached by a 14-km narrow and winding road off the main highway so it is inaccessible to coaches and other large vehicles. Brewsters had just taken delivery of a special vehicle for disabled passengers and Noel became the guinea pig for trying it out. It was very successful. The journey was longer than we had anticipated, especially as we kept stopping to look for wildlife. We had a new driver who was another mine of information to the extent that he never stopped talking! There were two hot pools, heated to about 40 degrees, and one cold pool. We all went swimming with the exception of Noel. He sat in his wheelchair at the side of the pools – the only person in the entire place with his clothes on! The swimming was lovely and the contrast between the hot and cold was very stimulating. There was a restaurant by the pool and we had dinner before our journey back. It was quicker than the outward one but just as verbal.

Travelling from Jasper to Kamloops the next day we had to pass Mount Robson, which is the highest mountain in the Canadian Rockies at a height of 12972 t. It is very frequently concealed by clouds but those gods were around again and we had a perfect view in brilliant sunshine. We stopped in a café nearby where we were able to enjoy the mountain and eat their speciality, cinnamon doughnuts.

By lunchtime, we had reached Dutch lake (the name is a corruption of Deutsch after the German settlers in the area). This was rather different. The landscape was less mountainous and there were huge areas covered with water lilies. An old paddle steamer takes groups on trips around the lake but we decided that we would just sit in the sunshine and enjoy our surroundings.

Swift Creek was a place on the river where the salmon come to spawn. There were many salmon there looking somewhat exhausted after their long trip of several thousand miles to this, their spawning ground. They would not make the trip back. Only the young salmon born here in the river would go back to the sea. The old ones would die. The bed of the river was made up of many coloured rocks and it was easy to see the fish against this background.

As we got closer to Kamloops the scenery changed quite dramatically. Gone were the snow-capped mountains, the thick coniferous forests and the rushing streams. Everything began to look much drier. This area is a continuation of the Sonora desert in the United States.

We were staying at the Thompson Hotel in the centre of Kamloops. We took a walk around, down to the big train depot. The railway is obviously an important aspect of the town. We crossed a level crossing and went down to the river (I think it was the Fraser river). On the way back we met two people on horseback. One was a local ranger, the other was a very glamorous young lady whom we were introduced to – Miss Kamloops.

We ate at a big bar/restaurant called the Fogg n'Suds. The meal was excellent with the usual large portions, but what really impressed us was the selection of beers available – literally from all over the world. Our younger son, Roland, is a beer bottle collector and he has several hundred from many far-flung parts. We obtained a photocopy of their beer list to give him when we got back. Meanwhile we sampled some ourselves.

After one night in Kamloops, it was off to our final destination – Vancouver. The scenery continued to be arid and quite mountainous. We found the contrast attractive. There were many areas covered in plastic sheeting. Sheila informed us that they grow ginseng underneath and that it takes at least three years for the plants to mature.

Our first stop en route was a very English establishment called the Ashcroft Manor Teahouse. When Bob had put the wheelchair into the coach that morning, he had spotted that there was a nut missing. It was very efficiently repaired by the chef and the owner of the teahouse.

We drove on through the Thomson River gorge and the Fraser gorge; the latter was particularly spectacular with the river way below. We could see railways on both sides – the Canadian Pacific and the Canadian National. Occasionally we spotted one of those incredibly long freight trains.

Then we were on the freeway into Vancouver and we made our way to the Quality Hotel in Howe Street where we would spend the next three nights. We were given a rather palatial room; it had a huge bed and a lounge area with a settee and chairs.

Importantly, it also had shower facilities that Noel could use. Sometimes, even rooms which claim to be for disabled guests still have a shower above a bath which is something that he, and most other people with similar problems, cannot handle.

That morning on the coach, we had been presented with a special certificate; we were the people with the lightest luggage in the group. A claim to fame that we would often get I think. Although there is almost always assistance with luggage, we have to be prepared for an occasion when this might not happen, and I always make sure that I can handle pushing the wheelchair and handling the luggage single-handed. That might mean piling some of it up on top of Noel, but we do work it out beforehand.

We were to discover that Vancouver is the city that has everything. That evening we walked down to the beach, which was not far from the Quality Hotel. It was a lovely sunny evening and there were lots of people strolling about. How nice to have an amenity like that in a big city.

We ate at a restaurant called Tony Roma's just round the corner. One of their specialities was barbecued ribs – and they were good.

An introductory trip of Vancouver was organised for the following morning. This was merely a drive in the coach with only one stop. We went to Gas Town, China Town and the harbour area, places that we could return to for exploration later. It was intended that we should visit Stanley Park but thanks to a gas leak, it was closed. Plans were changed to visit the Queen Elizabeth Park instead. It combines recreational facilities such as tennis with beautiful ornamental gardens and an arboretum. There was a group of Chinese men and woman practising tai chi. On the site is the Bloedel Conservatory, a glasshouse with a wide range of plants and flowers. We took a walk around the park and the conservatory.

By 11am the trip was over and the rest of the day was ours to do as we pleased. We started off in some of the art galleries. Howe Street Gallery had a very good exhibition of African sculptures but the one we really liked was the Marion Scott gallery, which specialises in wall hangings, prints and stone and whalebone sculptures from Northern Canada. The embroidery and collage by Inuit artists was particularly good – so intricate and colourful.

Gas Town was the birthplace of Vancouver. In 1886 it was just a settlement of loggers' shacks and saloons. It got its name from a John Deighton who built Vancouver's first bar and who was nicknamed 'Gassy Jack' because he always told such longwinded tales. After a fire, which destroyed the original wooden buildings and boardwalks in the late 1880s, many of the brick buildings, which are still there, were built. The arrival of the Canadian Pacific Railway to the area about the same time resulted in its rapid development, as well as the fact that it was a staging point for Klondike gold prospectors. From 1900 it gradually declined as an area until the early 1970s when it was the subject of a civic development project and many original features were restored. There is a steam-clock at the end of Water Street, which emits whistles every 15 minutes and a powerful blast every hour. It is powered by underground steam pipes. We took a walk around Gas Town, which has a very pleasant traditional atmosphere and is home to a variety of shops and restaurants. Obviously, there were many visitors and we joined them to watch the performance of the famous clock.

We had told Edgar's family that we were visiting Vancouver and had arranged to meet them that evening. Nearly all the family came along – Angie, her son Jeffrey, his wife Andrea and their children Jeremy and Rachel, as well as her daughter Barbara and granddaughter Heather. They arrived at our hotel and we went by car back to Gas Town. They had booked a table for the nine of us at the Old Spaghetti Factory. It is one of a chain of ten in the western part of the country and they advertise themselves as not only restaurants but also 'living museums of Canada's colourful past'. This one had a full-size old tram in the centre.

It was an ideal location for us all with good Italian food. Considering that we had never met before, we all got on extremely well and it was a very pleasant sociable occasion. It was 22nd August. Noel's birthday is the 24th and the staff all sang Happy Birthday to him in advance. Photographs were taken, email addresses exchanged and we returned to the hotel after a very satisfactory 'family' evening. Angie died in 2006 but we still keep in contact with the others.

Vancouver, like most of the modern cities we had encountered on our travels, was easy to negotiate with a wheelchair. It was an early start the next morning to take the ferry over to Vancouver

Island. We were blessed with perfect weather again and really enjoyed the crossing. Before going to Victoria, we visited the Butchart Gardens, about 21km from the town. They were started by a Mr and Mrs Robert Pim Butchart. He was the general manager of a cement company and when this particular quarry had been worked out, they decided to landscape it. Today there is 55 acres of very beautiful horticulture. There is a Japanese garden, an Italian garden, a rose garden and a sunken garden, as well as a concert lawn with a stage, two restaurants and a coffee shop. We spent an hour and a half there and would have been happy to stay longer. Paved paths were marked with a disabled sign to avoid stairs and steep gradients and it was possible for us to see most areas easily. Everywhere there were sweeping vistas with an endless variety of trees, plants and flowers. To commemorate the 60th anniversary of the gardens in 1964, Ian Ross, the grandson of the original owners, created the Ross fountain. The water rises 70ft into the air and at night, apparently, is illuminated in sequences of brilliant colour. The Butchart Gardens are justifiably famous and we certainly enjoyed our visit.

We carried on to Victoria, which has a reputation for being very English. We would agree with that. It actually reminded us of Christchurch in New Zealand. The whole atmosphere of the place was very civilised and although there were plenty of people around, it felt calm and unhurried. There is an attractive harbour area where there were lots of street entertainers.

The Empress Hotel, another of the original Canadian Pacific Group, named of course after Queen Victoria, Empress of India, is a very imposing building indeed and looked like a rather special place for a beer. That was true. We sat in the Bengal Lounge and felt just as if we were back in the Raj.

There were Punka Fans on the ceiling, hand-painted silk murals and very comfortable leather sofas. Their curry buffet is renowned and had we wished to eat at that particular moment, it looked inviting. However, we just settled for soaking up the atmosphere over a beer.

Another impressive building is Government House and we strolled around the gardens there. It is a nice touch that in front of this traditional and rather pompous European-style building, there is a giant totem pole.

That evening the sunset was spectacular and we were able to appreciate it to the full as we returned to Vancouver on the ferry.

Saturday 24th – Noel's birthday – and he got the song again on the coach later in the day. Before that, though, we got up early and took the little ferry over to Granville Island. The island was created originally from material dredged from the harbour and deposited on False Creek sandbar. It was formerly the site of warehouses and foundries but it got a big facelift in the early 1970s. It is the site of the Emily Carr College of Arts and Design, a community centre, restaurants, shops and theatres. It also has a fantastic market selling a huge variety of fresh fruit and vegetables, bakery items, seafood and much more. The shops and stalls were heaped up with foodstuffs, some of the best we had seen anywhere on our travels. There were several fast-food counters. It was from one of these that we purchased our breakfast, which we ate on an outside terrace in the sunshine.

The marina gives the island a maritime feel with many shops devoted to selling all manner of items for boating. This was heightened that day by a special event of wooden boats sponsored by the Oarlock and Sail Wooden Boat Club of British Columbia. There is something special about wooden canoes and sailing boats – the craftsmanship was superb – and there were many boat owners and enthusiasts there to admire it.

We took the ferry back. The boats are small but with a bit of assistance boarding was possible. Another coffee outside in the sunshine then back to the hotel to get organised for our coach transfer to the second part of our holiday. We were off on a cruise to Alaska.

Chapter 7

North to Alaska

When we made our booking for Alaska, we were sent a brochure of shore excursions so that we could reserve our choices in advance. There was a wide variety, and they were keyed as to the physical level of the activity and whether it was suitable for a wheelchair.

There were not too many that had the actual disabled sign above them.

We were going to land at three ports – Juneau, Skagway and Ketchikan – and we made a choice for each one. There were several helicopter rides we could possibly have taken but they were rather expensive. As with all cruises, shore excursions are not included and have to be paid for separately.

At the time we decided that we would incorporate an Alaska cruise into our trip to Canada, I had expressed the view that I was not sure that I really wanted to visit one of the last wildernesses on earth on a cruise vessel – but given our circumstances it was probably the only way we were going to. It would take us up the Inside Passage, which is between mainland Alaska, and the many islands off the coast.

A coach took us from our Vancouver hotel to the cruise departure area, an impressive structure with a roof like lines of white sails. We were fast-tracked to our ship. The *MS Zaandam* is part of the Holland America line. It was only two years old and we quickly realised that it was a very attractive vessel. Its guest capacity was 1440 and it had a crew of 647. We had a disabled stateroom, which was located on Dolphin Deck 1, the lowest deck. The promenade decks with all the main amenities were on 4 and 5, but we were situated very close to the lifts. Doors everywhere opened and closed automatically as you approached them, so getting around was extremely easy. It would have been possible to use an electric scooter.

Leaving Vancouver we saw a spectacular view of the city. It was a lovely evening, and we stayed on deck for a long time just enjoying the scenery.

The *Zaandam* operated the system of first and second sittings for dinner, using the same table each evening. We were allocated at a table for six people, but that evening only two of them turned up. Prior to our meal there was a Welcome Aboard session by the cruise director, introducing the various people we would encounter on the trip and telling us a bit about the *Zaandam*.

The following day we were at sea. One of the features of the ship was its art and antiques collection, which had been purchased to the tune of 2.5 million US dollars. They had a brochure describing all the items, which were situated on all decks. It kept Noel and I occupied for a long time. There were many very good paintings in a variety of styles, excellent models and sculptures. One section concentrated on items from ancient Egypt. The Java Bar had all Indonesian work. It was better than many museums, and it was certainly a good orientation exercise as it involved visiting all parts of the ship.

Continuing the art theme, we went to an auction later in the day. These are a feature of American cruise vessels. We were certainly not going to be buyers and there was nothing that appealed to us anyway.

I sampled the swimming pool and the Jacuzzi. We had an excellent dinner when we were introduced to the captain. No doubt because it is Holland America, all the officers seemed to be Dutch and most of the crew were Indonesian. Very good and plentiful cuisine is, undoubtedly, an aspect of cruise and we were going to find this was no exception. The day finished with a musical show of a high professional standard.

On Monday 26th August at 1pm we docked in Juneau. During the morning we had been to a presentation about whales. Whale watching is a very popular activity on Alaskan cruises. It was a very misty morning and the visibility was poor.

We had chosen to go on the Mount Roberts tramway, a cable railway that went up to 1,800ft above Juneau and offered a panoramic view of both the town and all the areas around. That may have been true on a clear day but unfortunately it was so misty we could see very little. However, we visited the nature centre at the top where we saw a video about the rainforests and also a film *Seeing Daylight* made by the Tlingit.

There are several groups of native people in Alaska, the Tlingit being one of them. The girls who introduced the film were half Tlingit.

There are opportunities for walks at the top of the tramway but neither the weather nor the terrain was suitable, so we went down again to the town.

Juneau got its name from one of the first miners who came to the site. The United States had purchased Alaska from the Russians in 1867. The mountains around the town were rich in gold ore and it was part of the gold rush in the 1880s. The gold mines have long since gone but there are still some gold rush style saloons and the Last Chance Museum. The city has modern hotels, shops, etc. Reputedly a short distance outside it, you are in the wilderness of the Tongass National Forest but we did not see that.

What we did experience was what I described as a shopping mall for cruise ship passengers. Apart from the *Zaandam*, there were three other huge cruise vessels in the port, all disgorging their passengers onto the streets of Juneau. We walked around but I have to say we were not impressed.

When we got back to the ship we were told by people who had chosen it, that the whale watching boat trip had been very successful and they had seen lots of wildlife. We had not opted for a boat trip because being already at sea on the ship we wanted to see something on land.

That evening it was still raining and the visibility was poor. Our hope was that it would improve the next day when we were heading for Skagway.

Skagway is located at the northern end of the Inside Passage and it was a stop-off point for gold diggers making their way to the Yukon. They bought their supplies there before setting off on their long trek. It became a centre for saloons, brothels and gambling houses and had a population of 20,000. It was home to a super conman called Soapy Smith who was eventually killed in a shootout in 1898. After the gold rush finished it became the southern point for the White Pass and Yukon railway.

It was still raining when we went into Skagway. It was another shopping mall for cruise passengers, but it was a more interesting town than Juneau. Alaska is famous for its wooden craft items and we purchased a bowl made of spruce burls and a miniature totem pole.

We had reserved a trip on the Skagway railway. It is a narrow gauge line and the trains have old-fashioned parlor cars. We travelled in one, which was specially adapted for wheelchairs. The trip lasted three hours and went up to White Horse Pass and back. It climbs steeply past places with names like Bridal Veil Falls, Inspiration Point and Dead Horse Gulch to a height of 2,000ft. The weather cleared as we went up and we were able to enjoy the spectacular views. We travelled through two tunnels and some very high trestle bridges over deep valleys. Like all these old mountain railways, you wonder at the skill of the builders who had no modern machinery and contemplate the hardships they must have endured in the climate and terrain. There were lots of interesting wild flowers and shrubs alongside the railway. It was a thoroughly enjoyable trip and gave us some insight into the Alaska away from the coast.

As we came down towards Skagway, the mist and rain closed in again. We had chosen well going up into the mountains.

As I mentioned earlier, most of the crew of the *Zaandam* were Indonesian and that evening they put on a special show featuring traditional music and dance, which was most entertaining and made a nice change from the American comedian and magician that had featured in some of the other evening entertainment.

One of the highlights of any Alaskan trip is Glacier Bay. Known only to the native Tlingits who were seal hunters, it was first introduced to the outside world by an American, John Muir. The first shipload of tourists went there in 1883. There must have been many thousands since then! The bay is 65 miles long full of fjords and inlets. All around are views of giant glaciers. However, as in other parts of the world, the glaciers are receding and plant life is gradually establishing itself.

In the morning it was still very misty and we could hardly see the shore. We were not being very lucky with the weather. Fortunately, as we got further into the bay it cleared, and there was even a glimmer of sunshine. The scenery was certainly spectacular.

Back on the deck later in the afternoon it was time for a bit of whale watching. The rain had almost stopped and we saw some orcas, some sea lions and some hump-backed whales. In the photographs they looked a bit like dark triangles on the surface of the sea – but at least we could say we had seen some bits of whales.

When we arrived in Ketchikan the next day we had to disembark on a tender.

It was somewhat more complicated for a wheelchair user than just going down the ramp but it was accomplished successfully. My heart sank a bit when I saw there were already three huge cruise vessels in the port ahead of us.

The waters around Ketchikan are very good for fishing, especially for salmon. The first salmon cannery was built there in 1887 on the site of a former Tlingit Indian fishing camp. Then gold was discovered and silver and copper mined nearby so that by 1900 it was a busy mining town.

There was the choice of a lot of outdoor activities here – biking, walking, canoeing, fishing, snorkelling and someone able to take part in them would have been spoilt for choice. We had selected the visit to the Totem Bight State Park, which has the world's largest collection of totem poles. It is located 10km outside the city and involved an interesting drive through the Tongass National Forest. Originally an Indian campsite, it is on the shores of a lake. We approached it on a gravel pathway. Gravel is a difficult surface for wheelchairs but it was not too bad and certainly worth it for the surroundings. We were in rainforest with huge hemlock and cedar trees. The totem poles were as high as the trees with wonderful carvings of animals and birds. We also went into a traditional winter house for the clan. In severe weather all the villagers had their own sections within this large building.

When we got back to Ketchikan we strolled around the town. Once more the retail outlets catered for the cruise passengers. In all three towns we had visited, there had been many expensive jewellery stores. I asked the assistant in one of these what they did in the winter, only to be told they take their business down to St Marten in the Caribbean.

No doubt they then obtain their customers from the same cruise vessels.

One part of old Ketchikan that still remains is Creek Street. This is a curving plank road built on piling over Ketchikan Creek. It was formerly the red-light district of the town and no doubt did plenty of business in the gold rush days. One of the most renowned 'ladies' of the street was called Dolly and her house has been retained as a small museum. All the other houses are now shops.

Before we visited each of the three towns – Juneau, Skagway and Ketchikan – we were given leaflets with lists of the retail outlets and the expensive luxury items they sold. This did seem to sum up the commercial aspect of cruising, which really didn't interest us.

The next day was at sea. When we had sailed up this part of the Inside Passage on the way north the weather had been very misty. Now it was sunny and clear and we were able to enjoy the scenery we had missed before.

Our cruise was coming to an end, and packing was the order of the day. Having purchased quite a number of items en route, we would not be the lightest luggage now!

We passed the rest of the day eating a mixture of traditional barbecue food and Indonesian cuisine on deck. I had a swim and went for a mile walk round the deck (3.5 circuits).

What were our conclusions at the end of our Alaska cruise? The *Zaandam* is a very well appointed ship and from our point of view, very easy to get around. It offered a wide range of on-ship activities for those who wanted them They were non-stop all day – quizzes, bingo, bridge, basketball, yoga, various beauty presentations, sing-a-longs, dancing, etc etc. We went to the shows, which were variable in quality, though that must always be a matter of taste, drank in the bars – though not too extensively. Drinks are expensive on cruise ships and coming from Spain we were not used to paying a lot for our favourite red wine. The food was good and varied and available in one form or another all day from breakfast at 7am through to snacks at midnight. There was a wide choice of breakfast foods from the buffet. The dinners were at least four courses. I don't know how anyone could find more space for food at midnight but the option was there on the Lido deck.

People enjoy cruises for different reasons. Some will always mention the food first. Others enjoy the social nature of all the on-board activities. For us, although cruise ships make excellent floating hotels, it is the destinations that are important.

We have since met people who have said how much they enjoyed Alaska cruises. For us it was a disappointment. I think my first reaction was correct – a cruise ship is not the best way to experience one of the Earth's remaining wildernesses.

The following morning, a coach trip was organised. We had said goodbye to our guide Sheila before the cruise. This time we had Chris, the leader of another Travelsphere group. We all said how lucky we had been having Sheila whose personality had added to our enjoyment of the holiday.

On our first visit, Stanley Park had been closed by the gas leak. This time we were able to go in. There are many totem poles in the park but they are modern reproductions of original ones. It is a very beautiful area, especially in the middle of a city. Huge old trees were a feature and as it is quite high up, there were views all round.

We had another visit to Granville Island, this time via the bridge not the ferry. We watched a very entertaining escapologist street entertainer and bought smoked salmon in the market. Our final destination was Queen Elizabeth Park. We had visited it before but members of the other group who were now with us had not. It was Saturday afternoon and obviously a very popular place for wedding groups to have their photographs taken. We saw several arriving in white stretch limos.

At 3.30 we had to check in at the airport for our flight back to the UK. It was due to leave at 6.30 and actually took off at 7.10 thanks to a missing passenger who never appeared. We made good time and reached Heathrow early on Sunday 1st September.

Canada had been a huge success full of interesting experiences. The countryside in the Rockies is spectacular. People who had started off as strangers had been unfailingly friendly and helpful and Noel had been able to participate fully in so many activities.

The magic that is Fiji

Heading up to Kuranda in Queensland, Australia

Coming off the bum boat in Singapore

After tiffin in Raffles, Singapore

Leaving the Emerald via the goods entrance

Pushing a wheelchair on the Athabasca Glacier, Canada

Glacier Bay, Alaska

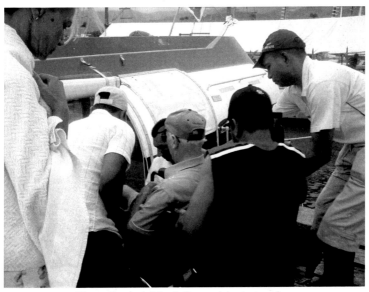

Transferring Noel from ship to tender

A view of our villa in La Fustera, Benissa, Spain

Noel and Martin by the bridge over the River Kwai, Thailand

Looking over Hong Kong from Victoria Park

Tiananmen Square, Beijing. Spot the picture of Chairman Mao

Our mobile home at Parc St. Vincent, Levignac de Guyenne, France

Special transport in Salvador de Bahia, Brazil

The pigeon at the top of the Empire State, New York

The scooter riders of Ho Chi Min City, Vietnam

A Canadian mirror lake

A Brazilian beer at Copacabana, Rio

Chapter 8

Dali and Picasso

Our Spanish home was in Benissa on the Costa Blanca. In the nearby town of Calpe there is a flourishing branch of the U3A (University of the Third Age), with a wide range of activities. All groups are run by voluntary leaders with knowledge or interest in their subject. Noel organised a painting course every Monday afternoon. Sometimes they met at our house or the home of one of the members. On many occasions they went out and painted by the sea or in the countryside. I was a member of a creative writing group.

The U3A also organised trips to various locations in Spain.

We had our villa built back in 1980 and it was our holiday home until we came to live here 12 years ago. During our many vacations in Spain we had visited most parts of the country, but that was when Noel was able-bodied.

In February 2004, U3A had a four-day trip to Figueres and Barcelona and we decided to join it.

We left Calpe by coach on Wednesday 25th in rather heavy rain and drove up the motorway to Figueres on the Costa Brava and not too far from the French border.

We stayed at the Hotel Presidente right in the centre of town. It was a large, modern building and we had an excellent dinner.

Figueres was the home of Salvador Dali. The following day we went to visit the Dali Teatro-Museo – so called because it was originally a theatre and was converted as the home for much of his work in 1974. The items there span his career from 1904 to 1989.

Surrealism is obviously well represented but there are also examples of other more conventional styles. The large central area is dominated by a vintage car with a huge sculpture of a woman standing on the bonnet and there is a column right up to the top of the building with a sculpture on top. In the background is an enormous surrealistic mural. The walls around, covered with thick foliage, have golden nude figures at intervals and behind these walls are galleries on four levels filled with hundreds of paintings and sculptures. The famous red leather sofa supposedly based on Mae West has its own display area.

Unfortunately for Noel, the only part of the museum he could access was the large central area on the ground floor. However, he was able to see a good selection from there. I explored the upstairs galleries. Whether you like the work of Dali or not, he was an excellent artist and the presentation in the Museo was quirky and very original − difficult to describe adequately in words. We both enjoyed it.

Figueres is a typically Spanish town, not very large and from our point of view, easy to get around.

Late afternoon Noel and I went on our own to visit two other museums in the town. The first, called the Emporda, housed an interesting collection of local items and paintings. The second, Museu del Joguet de Catalunya, was devoted entirely to toys. There were more than 4,000 items − Meccano, dolls, trains, cars, etc etc etc. Whatever plaything you think of, it was probably there. Some of them had belonged to famous people like Dali and Miro. It was inaugurated in 1982 and won a national prize of popular culture in 1999.

Both these places had a disabled entrance and a lift to the upper floor.

There is another Dali museum at Port Lligat. It is made up of a number of fishermen's huts where Dali and his wife Gala lived. The plan had been to visit this but our organiser discovered that it would be closed until March. Port Lligat is near the town of Cadaques, where Dali grew up. We drove to Cadaques through attractive mountain scenery.

It is by the sea and there is a walk along the coast to Port Lligat. It was certainly not a wheelchair-friendly town and the weather was very cold. We went for a short walk then Noel decided that he would prefer to sit in the coach. I went to look at the old town and up the hill to the church. In different weather I think we would have appreciated it more, but on a cold February morning it was rather bleak.

The coach then took us to Barcelona. Noel and I had been to Barcelona before but only for a short visit. This was a chance to get to know it better. We were dropped off by the Columbus statue and walked up the Ramblas to the Plaza Catalunya. The Ramblas is always a pleasant experience, especially the wonderful flower stalls.

Our hotel was the Pere VI. It was in a rather run-down part of the city, an old industrial area, but the hotel itself was very nice. Unfortunately, it was not really an easy walking distance from the city centre.

However the following day we had an organised trip. We went to the Sagrada Familia. The construction of this church began in 1882 and a year later Antoni Gaudi was appointed director of the project. He worked on it until his death in 1926. It is still not completed and relies entirely on private donations. The façade features the most incredible carving. We walked through the inside where there was scaffolding in place.

Work is still proceeding and nobody knows when it may be finished – or whether it ever will be finished. But finished or not it is a fascinating building.

Barcelona is the city of Gaudi. Evidence of his work is everywhere. The Park Guell has curved benches, the backs a mosaic of multi-coloured pieces of pottery. There is a wonderful lizard composed of the same material. The park is high up with great views over the harbour.

We would have been happy to spend much more time at each of these locations, but the coach was there to drop us back in the city centre.

We had another stroll down the Ramblas and some lunch in El Corte Ingles, which is the major department store group in Spain.

After lunch we went to the Picasso Museum, close to the city centre. It houses a very comprehensive collection of his work from his earliest periods through to the cubist paintings, for which he is so well known. They were all very well displayed in a most attractive old building. He is an extremely good artist and it was interesting to see so many examples in one place and to appreciate how his style evolved.

Our final visit of the day was to the Olympic Stadium, which enabled us to see yet another part of the city.

It was Saturday evening and the centre of Barcelona was buzzing with people. We had a meal organised at a restaurant close to the Plaza de Catalunya.

Sunday morning we were due for a guided tour on foot through the Gothic Quarter. We would very much have liked to see the inside of the Palau de Musica, another example of the genius of Gaudi, but tours were booked up for the entire day. Roman remains told us something about the antiquity of the city. The Ajuntament (town hall) was very impressive and we spent some time walking around there. It was rather like a grand church in the main chamber with tapestry wall hangings and chandeliers.

Our visit to the cathedral was well timed, between two masses. Like most Catholic buildings, it is very large and ornate.

More interesting was the activity on the plaza in front of the cathedral. Every Sunday people take part in traditional Catalan dancing. Anyone can join in and it is very informal. They put their coats and bags in the centre of the circles and just dance around them.

We took a cab back to the hotel and relaxed prior to our evening meal. Once more it was organised in a city centre restaurant, this time in a lovely old traditional building. The only snag was that we were to eat downstairs and the way down was a narrow spiral staircase. Our friends still talk about Noel being carried down by the waiters and all the people in the bar applauding them when they carried him up again.

As football fans we enjoyed our final visit the next morning. We went to the Camp Nou stadium, home of Barcelona FC. It looks impressive on TV but it looks even better when you are standing in it. The museum has a fascinating collection of football memorabilia related to the history of the club. Like all the big teams, there was a shop where we purchased a few goodies for our grandsons.

The weather was much clearer as we travelled back. We are used to relatively warm winters on the Costa Blanca but it had certainly been cold that bit further north in Figueres and Barcelona, though for the record that Monday night was the coldest one in more than 20 years recorded in Alicante province.

Chapter 9

The Big Apple

It was a Saturday some time in March 2004 when we were reading the Daily Telegraph that we spotted an advertisement for a flight to New York and hotel accommodation in the city at a very reasonable price. We had often said we would like to go there and Noel's reaction was 'ring them up now'. I did just that. The man at the other end was most helpful. I explained that we would need accommodation that was suitable for a disabled person. He checked things out and suggested a different hotel to the one that they were offering, which would be more suitable. We decided on dates – April 24th to 29th – and made the booking there and then.

April 24th was a Saturday. We got a morning flight from Alicante to Gatwick. Our daughter-in-law Isobel and grandson Alexander met us at Gatwick and drove us over to Heathrow, where we boarded a British Airways flight at 18.10 bound for JFK, New York. It was a pleasant, uneventful journey and we arrived about 20.00. The level of assistance at JFK was the best we had experienced anywhere. An airport employee met us at the plane, wheeled Noel through immigration without any of the usual American queuing delays, waited while I collected our baggage (only one smallish item), asked if anyone was meeting us. When I said we needed to get a cab, he came outside the building to the cab rank and organised our transport. I know they get tips for everything in the States, but he was certainly well worth it.

At that time in the evening it was a relatively quiet drive down the freeway and into the city. Our hotel was the Comfort Inn, Central Park West, one of the Choice Hotels group.

Located on West 71st street, a quiet location, it was quite small but very friendly. Our room was adequate with sufficient space for a wheelchair although it did not have disabled bathroom facilities. However, we were only there for four nights so that was no great problem. As I have said before, if the shower is not possible, one can always wash.

We woke up to a nice sunny morning. The breakfast room in the hotel was small and the choice limited but it was fine.

Central Park was at the end of the road and after breakfast we walked down there. (I am going to talk about 'walking' a lot in New York, which actually means me pushing the wheelchair.) The whole place was full of Sunday morning activity. Lots of cyclists were on the road and a 4-km run in aid of a cancer charity was in progress in the park. We were told that 8,000 people were taking part and there certainly were a lot of them of all ages.

The park was beautiful with masses of trees in blossom. It was a lovely atmosphere of people enjoying their Sunday morning. We went through to the other side to the Metropolitan Museum. What a fantastic place. If we had tried to see everything in there I think it would have taken the whole of our four-day trip. Apparently, a quarter of a million objects are on show at any one time. It is just enormous and everything is so well displayed. We made a point of seeing the paintings and also enjoyed the African and South American sections. The special feature at that time was the Byzantine exhibition with many examples of art from the Orthodox Church.

After some refreshment in their café, we went on to the Guggenheim. Frank Lloyd Wright was the architect and it was completed in 1959. The inside of the building is very impressive, built like a spiral with galleries off to the side. There are seven levels, which are reached by walking up the spiral or by taking an elevator to the top and walking down. It had a special access for wheelchairs and the slopes were gentle. However, we were disappointed and felt that in many respects the building was more interesting than the exhibits in it. However, modern art – especially of the kind that uses blocks of wood, areas with special lighting and video presentation – is very much a matter of individual choice. Some of the items were interesting, others made one raise the question 'Is this really art?' More conventional is the Thannhauser Collection, a permanent one, which features well-known impressionist and modern artists.

At this stage the weather began to deteriorate and it got much colder. We took a walk down Fifth Avenue. Being Sunday the big stores were closed, but we had a quick look round the Rockefeller Centre before making our way back to the hotel.

In the evening we found a very good Italian restaurant called Sambuca in West 72nd street, the next one to our hotel. It was busy and the food was excellent but we discovered that drinking wine in the States is quite an expensive option.

On Monday morning it was wet. Our intention had been to start the day with a trip up the Empire State Building but the top of it was in the clouds We took a cab down there and bought tickets, hoping that we would be able to use them later in the day.

Walking round in the rain was not a great option either. Sitting in a wheelchair one can get very wet, unless well covered over. So we decided that a bus trip around the city would be a good idea. They started and finished in Times Square. Similar to many cities they were open-topped buses and people who wanted to sit upstairs in the rain were given plastic capes. Noel could not have gone upstairs anyway and in view of the weather we were more than happy to stay below. Passengers can leave the bus at any stop and continue the trip on another bus when they wish. We just stayed on and went round the full route. There was a commentary and we were intrigued at the number of references to films that had featured the various locations. It was a good way to get an overview of the city and Noel still has one of those plastic capes with Gray Line bus tours on it.

We had a lunchtime snack in a deli on Broadway. New York delis certainly have a great selection of good food.

The rain had stopped and the sky was clearer. The top of the Empire State had reappeared. You enter in a large hallway draped with the stars and stripes and travel very rapidly by one of the elevators to the top. It is 1250ft high and has 102 floors.

Even though the visibility was not fantastic that day, we had a great view of the city. I took loads of photographs in all directions but my favourite is of a pigeon that landed on the parapet right in front of me. I know birds can fly high up but I was surprised to see him. There he is, silhouetted against a background of distant skyscrapers.

That was a lucky break in the weather because it started to rain again. We went back to the hotel with Noel clad in his cape. Our meal that evening was in an Argentinean restaurant on Columbia Avenue.

Tuesday and happily the rain had gone. Circle Line Cruises have a trip right around Manhattan Island and we decided that we would spend the morning doing that.

We took a cab down to Battery Park right at the bottom of Manhattan, the starting point for the trip. It lasted three hours and circumnavigated the 35 miles around the island.

We passed Ellis Island, where all the immigrants to the United States were processed in the past. The first one to disembark here arrived in 1892 followed by another 16 million over the next 40 years. It is reckoned that half the population of the United States can trace their roots to an Ellis Island immigrant. It is possible to visit the island and the museum on it, but our trip did not give us this option. We sailed by the Statue of Liberty. It is a symbol we have all seen many times on film and it was rewarding to pass close to the real thing. We went under seven big bridges including the dramatic Brooklyn Bridge. The trip gave us another view of some of the major buildings we had seen from the streets. It was a very worthwhile outing and another way of getting an overview in a short time.

Leaving the boat, we took a cab to Greenwich Village, which we had seen briefly from the bus the day before and wanted to explore in more detail. That has certainly been the location for many films – just think Woody Allen for starters. English colonists who settled there at the end of the 17th century gave it the name after Greenwich in London. It was very different to the other parts of the city with lovely traditional brownstone houses and lots of trees. We wandered around and had some lunch in a French restaurant.

The son of one of our friends in Spain lived in New York and we had arranged that we would meet him and his girlfriend for dinner that evening. That part of the city, which had been the meat packing area, was in the process of being changed into what could best be described as yuppy, with restaurants and designer boutiques – rather like Covent Garden in London. It was here that we had arranged to meet them at a restaurant called Pastis. We had plenty of time and it was within walking distance of Greenwich Village.

We arrived early, so we had a drink in another bar. New Yorkers eat earlier than we are accustomed to do in Spain and we duly met them at about 6.30. Gareth and Kathryn both worked in advertising and were fairly typical of the clientele of the area. Pastis was a trendy, busy restaurant. We had never met them before, but we had both worked in advertising in the past, and we had a very pleasant evening.

Wednesday was our last day in New York and we still had not visited one of our main aims – the Museum of Modern Art (MOMA). At that time it had been relocated from its original site to Queens. So we duly got a cab over there, only to discover that they were closed on Wednesdays as well as Mondays. My pleas fell on fallow ground. There was no way they were going to open for us! That was a disappointment, but there was nothing we could do about it. Tomorrow we would be back in the UK

One of those places always associated with New York is Grand Central Station. It has featured in so many films, especially the clock that people meet beneath.

So find another cab and head from Queens to see it for ourselves. They say that if you stand there long enough all the world passes by. I don't know about that but it is a very impressive place, almost more like a cathedral than a railway station. It dates from 1913. The roof is millions of stars and features a medieval zodiac sign. Its design was modelled partly on the Paris opera house. It was busy and well worth a visit, even though the clock is smaller than one would anticipate.

The only store we had visited so far was Macys, which we found a bit disappointing. Time to walk down Fifth Avenue again and look at some of the others. We walked up and down Fifth Avenue a lot of times in our four days. Sachs was much more up-market and warranted a stroll around. If I had seen something in the fashion line that I really liked my credit card would have come out, but I didn't like the styles too much that year. They were all a bit candy coloured. So we just enjoyed looking.

We had some lunch in Trump Tower. It is a rather glitzy building with lots of glass and marble. There are shops and restaurants and being in the middle of Fifth Avenue at lunchtime it was busy.

We were still disappointed about MOMA and decided that we would go to the Witney Museum of American art instead. Gertrude Vanderbilt Whitney started it with her collection in 1929. The outside of the building is quite stark but there are some excellent galleries inside and we were really pleased that we went. There was a very good selection of work by American artists such as Edward Hopper, Jackson Pollock and many more.

Just time to walk back across Central Park before we had to head to the airport. We really loved the park. It was a slightly longer walk than we intended because we went the wrong way but we did make it back to the hotel in time for our cab.

I have mentioned cabs many times. It was our best way of getting around the city. The subway was not possible. Buses might have been but for such a short visit it was hardly worth getting to know the routes. Cabs were not expensive and relatively easy to obtain. Sometimes it involved standing in the road for a while trying to hail one at busy times, but we were not in that much of a hurry. We had cab drivers of all nationalities and they were all ready to assist with putting the wheelchair into the boot of their vehicle. Some of them were really interesting to chat to.

Getting around the city did not present any problems. There were ramps at every intersection, even if there were an awful lot of intersections. Restaurants were all accessible and had disabled toilets. As with everywhere we had travelled, there were always people ready to hold doors open, etc.

When we got to JFK I bought some perfume in the Duty Free and a book called *Forever* by Pete Hamill in the bookshop. Pete Hamill wrote for most of the New York newspapers at one time or another. His book is a fantasy about a man who can live forever provided he does not leave the city and it tells the story of New York from the 1700s to the present day. Having just been a visitor, I found it absolutely absorbing and one of the best reads for a long time.

We arrived back at Heathrow at about 9am. In contrast to JFK, the poor level of assistance we were offered appalled us. Noel's wheelchair had been put in baggage rather than being immediately accessible when we left the plane and we had to wait for ages for an airport employee to bring another one. I will come back to discussing Heathrow again later. We have had experience of many airports around the world and it rates the lowest.

I hired a car at the airport and we spent the May Bank holiday weekend in England. There was one very special event – our daughter Claire had just adopted her daughter Lauren, and we met her for the first time. Then it was back to Spain again where we both agreed that our trip to New York had been a great success.

Chapter 10

Bangkok to Beijing

December 1904. We were flying from Alicante to Gatwick to spend Christmas in England. The cabin crew handed out copies of the Daily Mail, a paper we never normally read. In it we spotted an advertisement by a company called Voyana for a cruise to the Far East.

Earlier in the year Noel had expressed an interest in a trip to China, but when I spoke to the travel agents they advised against it, saying it would be quite unsuitable for anyone in a wheelchair as all the temples and historical sites often had long flights of steps and many of the towns would be very difficult. We had also contemplated perhaps taking a tour that incorporated Hong Kong and Thailand.

The cruise that was advertised ended with three days in Beijing and also visited Hong Kong and Shanghai. It started with three days in Bangkok and incorporated Singapore, Vietnam and Japan. It sounded perfect for what we wanted.

When we got to England, we telephoned Voyana and booked up immediately for the following November. Now that was really planning ahead for us!

Voyana turned out to be an excellent travel company. The ship involved was the *Diamond Princess*. We soon had a disabled stateroom booked and we were kept regularly updated on cruise details.

We carried on with our usual lifestyle, living in Spain and visiting England again for a month in the summer, until eventually November 4th arrived. The flight to Bangkok was scheduled for

22.00 from Heathrow. We were able to get a flight from Alicante to Heathrow that afternoon.

The Alicante flight came into Terminal 1. Our flight to Bangkok was from Terminal 4.

I have indicated before that Heathrow is not exactly our favourite airport. We had a large case, which I could pull behind me. I pushed the wheelchair with my other hand and Noel had a smaller case on his lap: manageable over a short distance, but not the interminable trek from Terminal 1 to 4. There are phones where one can ask for assistance. I did so and a porter arrived. He took us to the station where it is necessary to take an underground train and I was astonished when I was asked to pay £8 for the service. He alerted someone to meet us at the Terminal 4 station, who was there when we arrived. Service of a sort, but it is the first time we have had to pay for it!

The flight to Bangkok with Quantas took off at 22.00. Something strange happened to me. I walked along the plane to the toilet, and the next thing I knew I was lying on the floor with two crew members leaning over me. I never faint so I have no idea why I did then. As I fell I had broken the side of my spectacles. I then proceeded to be sick on my clothes and was given a pair of club-class pyjamas, several sizes too large, to wear. Noel was unaware of all this as he was asleep in his seat. I was fine afterwards. I'll never know what caused it but it did make me think about one's responsibilities as a carer. Suppose it had been serious and I had ended up in hospital – what would they have done with Noel? However, it didn't happen.

We arrived at 15.45 in Bangkok, Friday having merged into Saturday on the flight.

I felt very elegant in my pyjamas, but I doubt if anyone really noticed. They were a bit like a very baggy jogging suit.

It took quite a long time to sort things out at the airport. There were lots of representatives of different travel companies there. By the time we eventually left on our Voyana coach, it was raining and quite dark.

We were staying at the Marriot Resort Hotel, a short distance out of the city centre by the river. A bit like when we arrived in Fiji, it was obvious that the gardens were extensive and beautiful and we looked forward to seeing them in daylight the following morning.

It had been a long two days joined into one but it was still only early evening in Bangkok.

By crossing a small road in front of the hotel it was possible to enter an indoor shopping centre. There was a flight of steps into it but plenty of willing helpers from the hotel carried Noel and his chair up them.

I was a bit surprised that the first shop in there was Boots the chemists. It really is a small world these days. There was the ubiquitous MacDonald's, KFC and Pizza Hut, but fortunately also a Thai market and lots of other more interesting shops and restaurants. We ate in one called Sizzlers (not a very Thai name, it must be said). It was very popular with local people and the food was good.

At 20.15 it was off to bed. We were looking forward to seeing more of the hotel and the city the next day.

Voyana had some trips in Bangkok included in the price of the trip. The morning started with temples. The first one, Wat Trimitr, was in the middle of some narrow city streets and was the site of a solid gold Buddha. This one would have been totally impossible for Noel, so he stayed in the coach while I climbed up a steep flight of steps to have a look.

The second location was more rewarding. There were several temples, again not very accessible, but it was easy to walk around the area and there was plenty to see. I went in Wat Pho, the temple with the reclining Buddha. He is gold and he is absolutely enormous, laying the length of the building. There were numerous Buddhas all around the site in various positions. We were told that these positions were linked to days of the week and the one on which you were born determined your Buddha's position.

It was very busy with Thai visitors. There were many schoolchildren all very smartly dressed in their various uniforms. A group of young girls were being taught Thai dancing, which certainly involves having an excellent sense of balance. They were all dressed in traditional clothes – white blouses, baggy red trousers and a turquoise blue tie round their neck, and they looked delightful.

Next we visited a gem factory with, of course, a retail outlet. We were to discover that if you went on an organised trip at some stage you would be taken to a place where it was hoped you would spend money – and no doubt earn some commission for the tour guide!

Thailand specialises in sapphires and rubies and there was some lovely jewellery, but our sole purchase was a small elephant. They are supposed to be lucky for good health.

As we drove from one place to another we were beginning to get a feel of the city.

This was a Sunday so it was going to be different to a weekday, but there was still plenty of traffic, including lots of tuk-tuks whizzing around. We realised that we were not going to take a ride on one. Noel might get in okay but there was certainly nowhere for a wheelchair. We noticed a lovely flower market, which we would like to have explored in more detail. It was obvious that negotiating the city with a wheelchair was not going to be easy. Businesses spill out on to the pavements, cars and mopeds are parked on them. But it certainly had to be worth a go.

Back at the hotel, we were able to do some exploring there. We had seen some of the grounds when we had walked over to a restaurant for breakfast, but we now realised how big it was. In traditional Thai style, it had lots of open spaces and walkways in gardens full of tropical plants and trees. There were little bridges crossing over water features. Small buildings in the grounds were examples of Thai architecture but the main hotel was several storeys high. The outdoor swimming pool was elegantly landscaped and looked most inviting. Down by the river there were outdoor bars and cafes, all part of the hotel complex. The main hotel building contained many lovely items of traditional art and craft. It really was a delightful setting. We have stayed in a lot of big hotels in various parts of the world, but this certainly rated as absolutely top class.

After a snack lunch we thought about ways of going back into the city centre to explore more on our own. There was a pier at the rear of the hotel and a ferry ran regularly down the river but it was quickly obvious that it was totally impractical for a wheelchair, as they were very small boats.

Our next idea was to get a taxi, but before we could do so, down came the rain. We were in the tropics, it was afternoon, and it really threw it down. We realised that it would be stupid to try and walk around the city getting soaking wet and we were there for another day.

So we explored the inside of the hotel instead. We looked at the shops and bought our granddaughter a tee shirt with jungle animals all over it. We had a cocktail in the Elephant Bar.

By then the rain had eased off. We were quickly discovering how charming Thai people are – ever ready to offer assistance with a smile. So it was no problem to get into the shopping centre again and out the other side. Our aim was a Thai restaurant in the square on the far side, where we had an excellent meal. I had shrimp cakes followed by chicken and ginger and Noel had sea bass with some very good sauces.

On the way back through the market area we did some shopping. Throughout our trip we planned to get our Christmas gifts for all the family.

A very good friend of ours had recently moved to Thailand. Molly was over 80 and after living in Spain for years she had moved to a residential home in England. She hated it. Her nephew had a house in Thailand and he arranged an apartment and a woman to look after her. We knew we would not be able to visit her on our short visit as she was some distance from

Bangkok but we telephoned her from the hotel. She had given us an incorrect number and Worapan, the receptionist, went to a great deal of trouble to find the correct one for us. Molly was not too happy as she had problems with her carer but was delighted to hear our voices and to know we were in the country. We thought we might return to Thailand some day to see her, but unfortunately, she died in 2006.

The next day we were due for a 6.30 start as a trip had been organised to the River Kwai. Neither Noel or I have any real interest in sites connected with wars and in a way felt we would rather have had more time to explore the city of Bangkok, but as it was scheduled we decided to go along.

Martin, another member of our group, was also a wheelchair user. His problems were completely different to Noel. His lower limbs were paralysed, so he was unable to walk. However, he was independently mobile in his chair and had been a disabled competitor in the London Marathon among other sporting activities. But he could not get into a coach so the tour operators had organised transport for him in a minibus with his wife Chris, and it was proposed that we should join them. Our guide the previous day had been very camp and somewhat over the top. A great enthusiast, he never stopped talking and was fond of frequently telling the same jokes. So we were quite pleased to have a quieter driver.

It was Monday morning and we saw the full extent of the traffic levels into the city. There was a several-mile traffic jam on the dual carriageway. Fortunately, we were going the other direction. It was a two-and-a-half-hour drive to our first location but it gave us a really interesting oversight of many aspects of the city and the areas beyond. The outskirts of Bangkok are a real mixture of old and new. Shiny modern towers stand side by side with shabby blocks of old flats. The roads are large multi-carriageways. All along them are the biggest advertising hoardings we had ever seen mounted on high scaffolding-like structures. The advertisers were mostly big Japanese, American and multi-national firms.

English usually accompanied the Thai language.

It's funny the little things you notice. I was fascinated by the fact that every garage or car repair place had racks with dozens of different designs of wheel trims. I asked our driver why. Apparently in Thailand, they are a sort of fashion feature and people change them regularly, a bit like people with their mobile phone covers.

There were small houses and businesses all along the sides of the road and we noticed that many people wore scarves over their faces to combat the high levels of pollution.

In one small town we saw a procession of school children obviously involved in a festival of some sort. They had bands with drums and lots of the girls were dressed as majorettes, American style.

After two and half hours, we duly arrived at the Jeath War Museum at Kanchanaburi. It is a realistic reconstruction of the huts the prisoners of the Japanese lived in when they were employed on the building of the Death Railway linking Thailand to Burma. In this hut there are many mementos of actual prisoners, including photographs taken at the time by Thais and prisoners themselves. Apparently in the early days, the Japanese did not object although it was later forbidden. There were also paintings done by prisoners, which illustrated the appalling conditions in which they lived and accounts written by ex-prisoners who survived. We found the paintings the most moving.

The Death Railway was 415km long, 303 of them in Thailand. Work started in September 1942. There were approximately 30,000 prisoners of war involved and more than 200,000 slave labourers from several Far Eastern countries, including India, Indonesia, Malaysia and China, as well as the Thais and Burmese. The prisoners were mainly from England, America, Australia and Holland, and 16,000 prisoners and 100,000 of the labourers died during the building of the railway from disease and starvation.

The leaflet about the museum, which is now run by the temple, has a section that reads:

'Dear Visitors. JEATH museum has been constructed not for the maintenance of the hatred among human beings, especially among the Japanese and allied countries, but to warn and teach us the lesson of HOW TERRIBLE WAR IS.'

Outside the museum were market stalls selling all the usual tat to visitors. Commercialism must prevail.

We then went on to the memorial cemetery also in Kanchangburi. In it were rows and rows of plaques commemorating British, Dutch and Australian servicemen who had died as prisoners of war. It is funded by the Australian government and is very beautifully maintained.

On to the famous bridge over the River Kwai. This was an exceedingly commercial site with a very busy market nearby and hundreds of people walking over the bridge.

Noel and Martin sat in their wheelchairs overlooking the river, while Chris and I walked on the bridge. It was just like a procession and we did not go right across. The whole place was just too touristy to feel any sense of the history associated with it.

Lunch was scheduled at a restaurant up in the hills and as we drove towards it, the rain started to come down with a vengeance. Our mini-bus driver took us right up to the entrance, which was a difficult one for anyone disabled. There were big puddles and the two men decided to stay in the vehicle and we could bring some food to them.

It was a huge place with a roof but open sides and there were buffet counters to help oneself to lunch. The food was not brilliant. Chris and I took some to the men before we sat down and ate in the restaurant.

There had been plans for the group to go for a trip on the railway after lunch, although doubts had been expressed about whether Martin and Noel would be able to get on the train. However, this was never proved. The rain was so heavy and the train was open topped, so the trip was abandoned.

We drove back the way we had come. Noel and I both felt that the day had not really been very rewarding but the journey had been interesting.

We got back to the hotel at about five o'clock, had a drink in the bar and a very good seafood platter in Sizzlers restaurant. Noel started his holiday cap collection with one from Bangkok.

He was tired and went to bed at about 9pm. I went for a swim. By then all signs of rain had gone and it was a lovely warm evening. The pool was lit up and it was quite magic.

Armed with my camera, I went for a walk around the hotel grounds. Electric bulbs were wound up the stems of the very tall palm trees, making them look like columns of golden lights.

Noel was fast asleep when I got back and I packed our cases. We had to put them outside our door by seven in the morning.

We both agreed that the Marriot Resort in Bangkok was probably the best we had stayed in and one we would like to visit again. Our room was first class. The whole environment was tasteful and luxurious. We didn't try most of the restaurants but the breakfasts were excellent with a choice of eating inside or outside on a terrace near the river. There was a selection of really good bars inside the hotel and in the gardens. The staff were delightful – always so welcoming and ready to offer any assistance that might be needed. We could have stayed longer but our cruise began the following day.

Having received an informative brochure from Princess Cruises some time ago, we had chosen whether we wanted to go on a trip at the various ports or whether we would do our own thing. Our cruise ship was the *Diamond Princess* and we were soon going to see what it was like.

Once more we were provided with a mini-bus with Martin and Chris. Our departure port was Laem Chabang, a two-and-a-half-hour drive from Bangkok. It was a different direction from our trip to the River Kwai, and we went out through what were obviously the more wealthy suburbs. The route was on two levels. The pay motorway was raised and the ordinary road was beneath. We travelled on the top level all the way.

When we left Bangkok the sun was shining but it soon became smoggy and very dull. We could see huge black skies ahead and eventually we were driving through heavy rain. Our driver did not know the port area well and it took him some time to find our location.

When we entered the reception area of the port building it was swarming with people and there were long queues. But we got fast-tracked again and were on the ship earlier than most people. We now realized that the *Diamond Princess* was indeed a very large vessel. Our stateroom was on Deck 10 and there were four more decks above us. There are only a limited number of disabled staterooms on each ship and when we booked we had been allocated an inside one. On our two previous cruises we had outside cabins and were not sure how we would feel about the total lack of windows. Was it going to feel claustrophobic? However, it was large with a big double bed and lots of mirrors. The bathroom was very well adapted with a walk-in shower. We were going to get very fond of our floating bedroom. It was rather like a cocoon. Once inside you had no idea of whether it was night or day and felt detached from the outside world.

Lunch seemed a good idea so we made our way to the self-service café. There was an excellent selection of hot and cold food. A Rumanian girl, a member of the crew in the restaurant, whisked Noel away on his wheelchair to help him choose what he wanted. That seemed like a pretty good omen for friendly helpfulness.

The rest of the day was about orientation and trying to remember which was the bow and which was the stern. The main atrium was very dramatic – it went through several decks and there were flights of stairs descending from the galleries at each level. From the huge lamps on the ceiling, through the faces of the lift shafts to the elaborately patterned floor, the mood was art deco and the effect was stunning. There were five main restaurants as well as the self-service area. Several bars were decorated with different themes. An indoor and an outdoor swimming pool awaited me.

The *Diamond Princess* operated two schemes for dinner. There was 'Traditional', which meant that you chose a first or second sitting and sat at the same table with the same people every day. There was also 'Anytime Dining', which enabled you to choose from four restaurants and eat between 6pm and 10.30. We had opted for this in advance. We had a drink in one of the bars and duly dined at 9pm There was a very good choice and given the capacity one could have had soup, salad, starter, main course and dessert. We do not possess the capacity, and usually opted for three courses.

The ship had a very large theatre. Our only access with a wheelchair was at the back but special places were allocated there. We went into the show briefly but didn't care too much for the singer, so we retired to bed. No need to think about rising early – we would be at sea the next day and there would be plenty of scope for getting to know our way around a bit better.

As with all cruises we received daily information under our door. One, the Princess Patter, was all about the various activities taking place on the ship that day; the other was about the ports we were visiting.

There were things to do from morn till night. You could play games, go to lectures, attend demonstrations, spend time in the health and fitness centre, go to meetings, etc etc.

Some of the items were intriguing. The Friends of Dr Bob and Bill W had regular meetings so did the Red Hat Society. Who were these people? I suspect if I was an American I might have known.

I spent part of my morning in the laundromat. Noel is a Mason so he went and joined in a meeting of Masonic folk on the ship. They were from the UK, America and Australia so that was interesting.

The sea was as calm as the proverbial millpond and it was very pleasantly warm.

There were several open decks for sitting and relaxing – and for walking or even running round should you feel inclined. I sampled the swimming pool with the open roof. The temperature was just right.

The *Diamond Princess* is an American vessel so all transactions are in US dollars.

We obtained some but did not know what the actual exchange rate was – no doubt Nationwide would tell me when we got our statement. We soon discovered the cost of drinks – the only item on board which is never inclusive. At 4.50 dollars for a glass of wine, we weren't going to imbibe too heavily.

After dinner we went to a very slick and professional show called *The Piano Man.* They had a caste of 22 entertainers and 30 musicians on the ship.

That night we put our clocks forward an hour. Altering clocks was going to be a very regular occurrence as we kept crossing time lines.

Our first destination was Singapore. We arrived about 11am, two hours later than was scheduled. This was when we first realised that because the *Diamond Princess* was so large it had to dock at container ports, which were usually some distance from city centres. To overcome this problem there were always hoards of shuttle buses to transfer the 2,500 passengers. Coming into port one was greeted by the sight of rows and rows of coaches lined up on the quayside. It looked as if every coach in the city had been requisitioned for the purpose.

It was the first time we had ever seen a container port. There were literally miles of containers lined up and hundreds of new cars.

Getting so many people off a ship is no mean achievement. Prior to disembarking, passengers were put into groups according to their choice of activities and it did take some time, especially when only one ramp was used. There was a special motorised device that pulled wheelchairs and their occupants up and down the ramp.

You will recall that we visited Singapore on our first round-the-world trip. As we had some knowledge of the city, we did not book an excursion. We went on the shuttle bus and then got a taxi.

Once again we were struck by the orderliness of the place. After the chaotic transport levels of Bangkok, it seemed positively provincial. Driving towards the city, we spotted a building that had not been there on our previous visit – the new Opera House. It looked like a superb piece of modern architecture.

We got the taxi driver to drop us off by Raffles Hotel. In need of some liquid refreshment, we went and sat in one of the courtyards with its relaxing backdrop of green trees and had a beer.

We strolled round a very swish shopping centre full of well-known international retail outlets. The same names now crop up all over the world. It is truly a global economy.

On our last visit we had enjoyed the works on display at SAM (Singapore Art Museum), which was a short walk away, so we decided to have another look. This time they had an exhibition of eight local artists. There were some interesting paintings in a variety of styles.

In need of a bit of afternoon refreshment, we decided we would have a Singapore Sling for 'old times' sake'. I didn't have the Indonesian dress on this time and we were not going to partake of tiffin.

Little India had also appealed to us on our first visit and Noel had bought a shirt that he really loved. Perhaps he would be able to find another one. We thought we knew exactly where we would find it, but when we got out of the taxi it was obvious that seven years down the line things had changed. The area seemed much bigger. We made our way through the very crowded covered market, selling all manner of clothes, but not the coveted shirts.

It was afternoon and down came the rain. It really poured and it took us a long time to hail a cab. Obviously everyone else had the same idea. Eventually we succeeded and we went back to the shuttle bus and on to the ship.

Every evening we asked to share a table for dinner. It was interesting to meet different people and the passengers were quite multi-national. (I will give you a breakdown of the nationalities later on.) That evening we were with two couples from Florida who had been respectively on 39 and 35 previous cruises. We came to realise later that this was in no way unusual and that many Americans seem to be addicted to this type of holiday.

What was notable that evening was what I always call 'the small world syndrome'. In other words, discovering that you have things in common with someone you have just met who comes from a completely different background to yourself. One of our fellow diners had family members who lived in the town in England where I grew up and her granddaughter went to my old school.

We finished the day on loungers out on deck. Evening, and the rain had gone. The air was balmy and much warmer than inside, where there was a definite tendency to overdo the air conditioning.

The following day we were at sea. A chance to laze around, read and swim. It was Remembrance Day and they had a special service on board, but I have to confess we did not attend. Noel met up with his Masonic mates again. Every day there were special features in the shopping area of the atrium and that particular day it was gemstones, which appealed to me.

Most evenings the dress code was what they described as 'smart casual' but twice during the trip they had a formal evening. Time to get out the posh frock and enjoy looking at what everyone else was wearing. There were a group of obviously very rich Russians on the ship and they were certainly not short of designer clothes.

Everyone assembled in the atrium and there were people standing at all levels. Freebie cocktails were served. The captain, who was English, welcomed everyone. I must say it was quite a glittering occasion.

That night the clocks went back an hour, which was a good thing as we were due for a 6am call the next morning.

We arrived at the port of Vung Tau in Vietnam and were going to visit Ho Chi Minh City. Prior to 1975 it was Saigon and during our visit we frequently heard it still referred to by its previous name. It was a two-and-a-half-hour drive and transferring everyone from the ship to the coaches was a somewhat lengthy and complex operation. We were on coach number 12.

It was a fascinating journey. The route was a dual carriageway road but not of the standard we had experienced in Thailand. The traffic was chaotic – trucks and cars and countless mopeds weaving their way in and out. In Thailand they drove on the left but in Vietnam it was basically on the right. Hooters are an integral part of the process. On either side of the road for the entire journey there were shops and commercial premises, many of them very small and primitive. People were selling cooked food, fruit and vegetables by the roadside, and it was again common for them to have scarves covering their faces to avoid the pollution.

As we approached the city, the number of mopeds increased even more. Everyone seemed to ride them. We saw whole families – including babies – perched on one machine, old grannies, men with their goods piled high. Helmets were scarcely in evidence though we did spot one girl riding pillion side-saddle carrying a helmet in her hand. We stopped at one intersection and when the traffic lights changed it was like a mass start race of mopeds from the right and the left.

There is a strong French influence on the architecture of the city dating from colonial days. We paid a brief visit to the Notre Dame Cathedral and the rather magnificent post office on the opposite side of the square, as well as a photo opportunity at the Reunification Palace.

The Museum of Vietnamese History gave us glimpses of the culture of the country from the earliest times. Rather like the Chinese, the centuries were divided into various dynasties. The guide at the museum did go into a bit more detail than perhaps we would have wished, but it was interesting information about a country whose history prior to the 20th century was unknown to us. While we were there, we saw a rather strange water-puppet show. We all sat around a pool inside the museum.

Our commercial visit of the day took us to a place where they made laquerware, which is a very traditional Vietnamese craft. There was furniture, vases, screens and all sorts of decorative items very skilfully and beautifully done. We purchased some small jewellery boxes as part of our Christmas present collection.

Lunch was at the Renaissance Riverside Hotel, a high-rise modern building. We had an excellent buffet and were entertained by a charming group of dancers accompanied by musicians. They wore colourful, traditional costumes and their movements were so graceful.

After lunch we went for a stroll along Dong Choi Street, the main shopping area of the city, which had a good variety of modern and more traditional retailers. Some silk ties were added to our gifts.

The pavements were not brilliant but it was relatively easy. As we walked around we kept encountering two rickshaw drivers. We were clearly not going to be clients but when we decided to cross one of the wide roads they came to accompany us. There were no real crossings and no little green men to tell you when to cross. So I wheeled Noel over with a rickshaw man on either side of us while traffic whizzed around. Our plan was to go down to the riverside but we realised it was not going to be possible so back we went with our rickshaw bodyguard. No doubt they were after a tip and we were pleased to give them one.

Something that I remarked on in the Caribbean struck me again here. The conditions in which many of the people seemed to live were quite primitive but everyone looked so neat, clean and well dressed. We really liked Ho Chi Minh City. It had a real buzz about it and the people were very friendly. The next day we were going to another part of Vietnam.

Nha Trang is a popular seaside resort for the Vietnamese. It has four miles of sandy beaches and many expensive hotels. Officially there is no industry and the main commercial activity apart from tourism is fishing. Its population is about 300,000.

The countryside around is rolling hills and green valleys with many farming villages.

Our ship anchored in the bay and everyone was taken ashore on tenders. It is sometimes stated that disabled passengers may not be able to disembark on tenders but in this instance it presented no difficulties.

We had elected to take a tour. Our first stop was the market. It was large and by the standards of this part of the world very well organised with permanent units.

The food stalls were absolutely fascinating. There was a lot of dried fish. Everything was very well displayed. I have to admit that there were some items that we had no idea what they were and some we knew what they were but certainly would not have wanted to eat them. It was obviously a market that catered for local shoppers as well as visitors to the town.

Nha Trang was an important place in the past with a long and interesting history. It was the centre of the ancient kingdom of Champa, which dominated the region from the 2nd to 25th century. Ruins of this civilisation have survived, most important of which is the Ponegar Cham Tower. It is a stone building at the top of a hill and is regarded as a holy place. Unfortunately, this was not accessible for Noel who stayed in the coach while I climbed up several flights of steps. The view from the top was superb, overlooking the Cai River where there were many fishing boats painted bright blue.

The Long Son Pagoda was equally inaccessible. It was founded in the 19th century and contained many murals and images of Buddha. An enormous white Buddha was situated on the hill behind the Pagoda which was built in 1965. Apparently it commemorates the Buddhist monks who protested at the abuses of the Diem regime in the early 1960s and set themselves on fire.

For me the striking feature of the Long Son Pagoda was the sheer commerciality of the place. We were besieged by women and children trying to sell us t-shirts, postcards, you name it.

Shoes have to be removed to enter this sort of religious building and they were practically removing them for us in the hope of getting a tip. I did wonder why there were so many children there. Why were they not at school? However, their hassling was very good-natured and they are generally friendly charming people.

At the Hong Chong Promontery, a house of the old traditional style had been reconstructed. Again a no-go for Noel but it was not particularly interesting. However, the view from there was enough to make the visit worthwhile with a vista of beaches and headlands.

The sort of commercial visit of the day was to Diem Tham Quan, which was an arts and crafts centre specialising in hand embroidery. There were about two dozen women dressed in traditional Vietnamese clothes, sitting in a workshop creating the most intricate embroidered pictures. To do work like this would require superb eyesight and very delicate hands. As well as seeing the pieces they were working on, there was also an exhibition of finished work. It was really very beautiful.

We finished off our visit to Nha Trang in a beach café drinking milk out of coconuts. The beach was soft sand and there were lots of trees – not the palm trees that you expect on tropical beaches. These were large old trees with gnarled trunks providing lots of shade and lots of character. It would have been lovely to stay there much longer but I did find time to take off my shoes, walk down to the water's edge and paddle in the warm sea. If only I had been able to swim. That is the snag of organised trips – you do not always have time to do some of the things you would like, but it had been an interesting visit to a pleasant town. What we had been told by travel agents was proving to be right – if you are disabled you have to accept the fact that some of the historical bits will not be accessible to you. I wonder how people who couldn't walk managed in the past. Perhaps they just stayed at home.

There were vast lines of passengers for the tenders back to the ship, but as usual we managed to do a bit of queue jumping.

Cruises offer you a taster of the places you visit. We liked our taster of Vietnam. Perhaps one day we might get the opportunity to explore more of that fascinating country.

The next day we were at sea, sailing north towards Hong Kong. There were usually lectures on board about the next port of call and we went along. They provide some background information.

There was a good jewellery sale that day and Noel bought me a gold chain from a retailer called Yard of Gold. They had a very wide choice and it could be cut to exactly the length you wanted, which is a very good idea. It had crystals and garnets in it and was perfect with the longer one he bought me in Greece years ago. I have never taken either of them off since they were first clasped round my neck.

Hong Kong is reputed to have the largest container port in the world and it certainly looked it when we docked early the next morning in rather heavy rain. The shuttle buses and the tour buses were all lined up again.

Hong Kong means 'fragrant harbour', which didn't really apply to this highly organised haven of containers and motor vehicles waiting export or import. From the 1840s, Hong Kong had served as a staging post and entry port between China and the West. It was occupied by the Japanese between 1941 to 1945. On July 1st 1997, Britain handed it over to Chinese control. It was definitely on our list of places to see, although we could only experience a fraction of it on this occasion.

We were booked on one of the tour buses. Our first destination was Stanley Market, reputed to be a great place for bargain hunters. It was indoor and very busy with tourists and locals. We got some t-shirts printed with our grandsons' names in Chinese script and a traditional *cheong sam* dress for Lauren, our granddaughter. We only had about 45 minutes and really could have spent longer – and probably spent more money!

Repulse Bay is the most beautiful beach in the city and the home of the wealthy. We just had a quick look on the way to

Aberdeen fishing village which is full of houseboats and fishing boats, some quite smart and modern, but many of them really ramshackle. They were originally situated in the main harbour but were moved to Aberdeen some years ago, as the main harbour is constantly being redeveloped. We went on a tour in a small boat. It was not easy for Noel to board and required several helpers but as usual it was achieved. The largest floating restaurant in the world – the Jumbo – is also situated there.

We were taken to a jewellery factory. I have to say that with only a day to see as much as possible of a place as fascinating as Hong Kong, 40 minutes spent there was really a waste of time. Noel stayed in the coach. Getting in was difficult and he really wasn't interested in making the effort.

The Peak Tram is a funicular railway. The track is 1.4km in length and rises from 28m to 396m above sea level. Fully computer controlled, the modern tramcars carry 120 passengers. It first started running back in 1888 when the trams were wooden and fired by coal-fired steam boilers. Although the rain had long since stopped, it was still a very misty day so we could not see too far in he distance, but we had a great view of all the high-rise buildings and the harbour. We went for a walk along the top.

After Bangkok and Ho Chi Minh City, the traffic levels were very low and the lack of private cars was striking. Our guide told us that only five per cent of the population own them. The tax on buying cars and petrol is very high. Mopeds and scooters are not popular. The public transport system is superb with lots of double-decker buses, a mass transit railway system and trams, which are also double-deckers. The whole transport system operates on a card system, which can be topped up like a phone card.

Nearly eight million people live in the city, about half of them in public housing. The apartments are very small. In some of the older ones it can be just one room for a whole family.

Many of the new buildings are of very innovative designs. They are gradually building further into the harbour so that what was on the shoreline is regularly being pushed back.

Unfortunately, we only experienced downtown from the coach. The streets were busy and colourful with lots of Chinese signs outside the shops and restaurants. On our drive back to the port, we went through Kowloon and the new territories.

One of the disadvantages of an organised trip is returning to the ship sooner than one would wish with so little time to see as much as possible. However, going independently to a large unknown city one could end up seeing less.

That evening we had a great bonus. I had purchased a set of postcards earlier in the day and many of them featured the city at night. We thought we were not going to see that, but the captain had been given special permission to leave Hong Kong via Victoria Harbour and it was better than any of the pictures. All the buildings were lit up along the waterfront, and we viewed this fantastic panorama from the 15th deck. We were all taking photographs and we could see the flashes of cameras belonging to people watching us from the shore. I suspect the *Diamond Princess* looked pretty impressive too.

Another day at sea and we were leaving the warm and balmy weather behind. It was cold and windy and the sea was getting very rough with really big waves. However the stabilisers on the ship meant that there was virtually no movement.

We've all bought items with 'made in Taiwan' on them but it is not a place that most of us know too much about. That was where we were heading. It is a large island 100 miles off the coast of China. The Portuguese named it Formosa, meaning 'the beautiful'. Twenty-two million people live there. It is sub-tropical and has a very high rainfall. One mountain area has ten times the amount of southern England and the port of Keelung has 80-90in. Most of the population is descended from Chinese settlers who arrived there in the 17th century. From 1895 to 1945 it was ruled by Japan. It reverted to Chinese control after the war and became the refuge for the Nationalist government under Chiang Kai Shek. Nowadays it is quite heavily industrialised. It imports raw materials and exports the finished products, especially computer components, electrical items and textiles.

We docked at the port of Keelung. Some of those 80in of rain was coming down but fortunately it soon stopped. We had opted for 'Taipei on your own', a chance to do our own exploring of Taiwan's capital city. The shuttle bus from the ship dropped us off by the Peace Park. We had decided that our first stop would be 101, the highest building in the world. There was a metro station by the park and we considered using it but there didn't seem to be facilities for getting underground by wheelchair so we opted for a taxi.

Standing 508m high, 101 is a very graceful building. The shape is not easy to describe. After a solid base, it is very slender with eight sections piled on top of each other up to a narrow pinnacle and a sharp point at the top. It is a very striking silhouette. We travelled by lift up to the 86th floor in 30 seconds without any consciousness of movement.

There is a circular indoor viewing gallery. We were there quite early in the day and it was not too crowded. When we go up high buildings it always seems to be misty, but despite that we were able to get a magnificent bird's eye view of the city and the surrounding area from the big windows all round. There is an open viewing gallery on the 91st floor and we went up there in the lift but realised that anyone who had to sit down in a wheelchair would not be able to see over the rails, so after a brief look we came down again. On the ground floor the building houses offices and a big indoor shopping centre.

Our next aim was the Chiang Kai Shek Memorial Hall. Chiang Kai Shek died in 1975 and Chinese communities at home and abroad donated funds to the government to build this memorial. It was completed in 1980. It covers 250,000m². Its architecture is traditionally Chinese and it is approached via a huge gateway and beautifully laid out gardens. The exhibition hall on the ground floor housed a wide variety of cultural relics and items relating to the life of Chiang Kai Shek. We were particularly intrigued by two huge American limousines, which he had apparently used. In an upstairs hall was an enormous bronze statue of the man. It was a bit like a shrine and many of the Chinese visitors seemed very reverent.

From there we walked to the Chinese craft centre. We were not exactly sure where it was so we covered quite a lot of ground and asked several people the way. Noel had to be carried up the steps. There was much to buy there but the quality was not very good so we did not become customers.

We walked on through Peace Park. It lived up to its name and was very pleasant with lots of trees and flowers. An outdoor café in the middle provided an ideal location for coffee and a snack. It was obviously a popular place with local people.

We enjoyed our day in Taipei. It is a big modern city, busy but in an orderly way with a nice atmosphere. There were no problems getting about and we enjoyed being free to go where we wanted, when we wanted.

The following day we were scheduled for Okinawa, an island lying half way between Taiwan and Japan. It is one of those names that everyone knows from World War II.

But we did not go there. Very high winds and rough seas made it impossible for us to dock. There were quite a lot of Japanese Americans on the ship and I imagine that they would have been very disappointed. I also felt sorry for all the coach operators etc who are involved when a ship like the *Diamond Princess* arrives. They must have lost a lot of income. So, unexpectedly, we had a day at sea. We were unaffected by the weather conditions but the movement of the boat was illustrated by the way the water in the swimming pools was flowing in big waves from one side to the other.

That meant that we had two consecutive days at sea. We went to an interesting lecture on Shanghai, our next port of call. I went to the film *Phantom of the Opera* in the afternoon. Noel didn't want to see it so he just sat in the Wheelhouse Bar and chatted to various people. Art auctions were held regularly and the paintings were displayed beforehand. We spent some time looking around them. There were some works by Leroy Neiman, an American artist who we liked and Noel spotted a book called *Leroy Neiman: Art and Lifestyle.* He wanted to get it, so when we were back home I went into Amazon website to find it. They located a copy at their second-hand bookstore in Portland Oregon and it was dispatched from there to England to be part of his Christmas present.

We are both keen tennis fans. I still play regularly. The Masters Tournament that year was in Shanghai. We were just approaching Shanghai and we watched the semi-final on TV in our room that evening.

Shanghai – a city with a fascinating history. It was a relatively small settlement until the end of the Opium Wars in the mid 19th century. From then on it grew to be one of the leading trading centres in the East. It was self-governing and it attracted fortune hunters, smugglers and inevitably gangsters. Soon it was famed for its luxurious and flamboyant lifestyle and the vices that went with them. The Chinese communist party was formed there in 1921 but it was not until 1949 that it was peacefully taken over by the communists. It went on to become China's biggest port and economic trading centre.

Its current population was 16 million and rising. According to our guide it was also home to eight million cyclists, not to mention a great many cars.

It was somewhere we were definitely looking forward to visiting and we were not going to be disappointed.

This time we had opted for a combination of guided tour and free time. We were going up in the sky again. The Jin Mao Tower, built in 1998, was the tallest building in China and the third tallest in the world at 421m. We had seen New York and Taipei from above. Now it was the turn of Shanghai. November 20th was a Sunday and the tower was choc-a-bloc with tourists. They were nearly all Chinese and we got the impression that some of the groups were on an outing from the provinces. It was a clear morning and we had a great bird's eye view of the two rivers, the Suzhou and the Huangpu. There were huge modern skyscrapers in all directions, many of very beautiful and innovative designs. In contrast, in one direction there were villas surrounded by trees. Part of their transport system is a magnetic aerotrain, and we could pick out the shiny silver roof of the station. There were sports arenas, bridges and roads. The road system of Shanghai is something else with its underpasses and overpasses. It was quite a crush in the viewing area, but we were able to move all round.

The part of the city where the tower is located was fields less than ten years ago. Now it is the home of some of the most impressive high-rise building you could find anywhere and a huge, very elegant telecommunications mast.

Then we headed for the old town, a very different Shanghai. It used to be a maze of narrow alleys but the streets have been widened. The market was very crowded with shoppers but it was quite easy to push Noel through. When we reached the Yuyuan Garden that became less true.

The Yuyuan Garden was built during the reign of Emperor Jiajing in 1559. It is of classical Chinese design and has 30 different pavilions linked by a maze of small footpaths and little bridges over ponds. One of the pavilions, the Huxining Teahouse, is reputed to be the model for the design on the willow pattern plates. With a wheelchair it was a fascinating nightmare and having started on the trip we carried on with innumerable helpers over the worst obstacles. Noel could not get inside any of the buildings but despite that it was certainly well worth the visit. It is very picturesque. The pools are full of carp. One particular ginka tree, which was enormous, was several hundred years old. I am always interested in anything to do with rocks – and there were many very carefully placed in their surroundings. Apparently, if they have a hole in them, they are very special. There were quite a lot of people but it still managed to be a delightful peaceful place.

The third famous area of Shanghai is the Bund. It is a riverfront promenade lined with graceful 19th century buildings.

This was where all the European capitalists of the time lived and ran their businesses. We passed by Nanking Street, which is the chief retail areas and there were hundreds of shoppers.

Our tour had shown us several different aspects of the city. It finished at a place that sold silk products. We could return when we wanted on the shuttle bus. We walked from there to the Shanghai Museum, a large circular building. We looked around the paintings section, which had fine examples of traditional Chinese art. Noel noticed that the lighting in the section varied alternately from light to darker. We thought this was probably to help preserve the paintings. The restaurant had finished serving lunches so we just had a drink. The museum shop had an excellent selection and we purchased an example of Chinese art and a fun book on learning Chinese (our grandson is doing so at school and he has since visited Shanghai on a student-exchange visit).

Outside the museum was People's Square. There were lots of people walking around or just sitting outside in the sun. Again a very pleasant relaxing atmosphere, quite surprising in a city that teems with people.

The Handicrafts and Silk Centre was well worth a visit. Noel had to be carried up the front steps and we used the goods lift to go from one floor to another. A silk blouse was added to the Christmas collection.

Noel had been in the wheelchair all day and it wasn't until we went to get on the shuttle bus that we realised he did not have his walking stick. That was a bit of a disaster but hopefully we would be able to buy another one somewhere. That somewhere was not the Handicrafts Centre but when we got back to the ship we went to the Medical Unit and they provided us with one, which we purchased later.

Shanghai had been a great day. We felt that we had managed to get a real feel of the place in the limited time available. We were achieving our original aim when we booked the cruise, which was to experience some of the great developing cities of the Far East. Although we were interested in the historical aspects, it was as they are today that really appealed to us. There were similarities and there were differences but all of them had been stimulating in their own way and there was one of the biggest, Beijing, still to come.

Our last bit of Shanghai that evening was to watch the tennis final on TV and a cracking match it was too.

The following day we were at sea, a much calmer one. The weather was getting colder as we headed north. I had the swimming pool all to myself, which made me very happy. We indulged in afternoon tea, the real traditional sort with scones, jam and cream. Then it was out with the glad rags for another formal evening.

Our last port of call was Nagasaki and for once we were able to dock right in the town as it has a very deep harbour. As everyone knows, Nagasaki was one of the two cities destroyed by an atomic bomb at the end of World War II. It was not the originally intended target. After Hiroshima the Americans were going to bomb Kokura, but due to haze and clouds they headed to Nagasaki instead. Forty thousand individuals died instantly. It has all been rebuilt, the only reminders of the past being the Peace Park and the Atomic Bomb Museum.

We decided to visit the Peace Park, which is located near ground zero, the centre of the blast that destroyed the city on 9th August 1945. A huge statue and a variety of other pieces of sculpture dominated the gardens. One corner was filled with garlands left by visitors, many of them consisting of origami birds.The coach that had taken us there drove up to the top of the hills overlooking the city so we had an overview. It was green and pleasant with no very high buildings. In the era when Japan closed its borders to the rest of the world, Nagasaki was about the only place where foreigners were allowed. It is very hilly, rising steeply from the harbour.

We did not visit the Atomic Bomb Museum and decided we would walk around and explore. However, we were defeated by the steepness of most of the roads. It was just too much hard work pushing Noel up them. So we stayed down by the harbour. Viewed from the end of a road, the *Diamond Princess* looked incredible. With its 14 decks, it appeared more like a multi-storey building than a ship.

We spent the remainder of the afternoon on board. Groups of Japanese business people were being shown around.

The *Diamond Princess* had been built by Mitsubishi in that very harbour 18 months previously. In the early evening there was a presentation of plaques between the captain and the publicity director of Mitsubishi. I suspect it was the first time the ship had been in the port since its completion.

Some children from a local nursery school gave us a show in the theatre. They were all aged between four and six years, dressed in traditional Japanese costumes. It was absolutely delightful.

As we sailed out in the evening the local high school band played and loads of local people lined the shore to give us a big send-off. After all those container ports it made a very pleasant change.

Our last day at sea. After enjoying all the excellent food we had eaten during the trip, we attended a demonstration by the chief chef, an Italian. We went on a tour of the galley. We learned that most of the food for the trip is loaded at the beginning to be placed in special storage areas. (This was a bit different to the *Emerald* in the Caribbean when Noel always seemed to be entering and leaving the ship as food supplies were coming in.) They gave us a leaflet with details of how much of certain foods were prepared every day. The bakery used an average of 1,700lbs of flour, and 7,000lbs of fresh fruits were served. Coffee ran to 470 gallons. Fifty-two men had the sole task of feeding the dish-washing machines. A daunting enterprise – and I couldn't help wondering how much food got wasted, especially from the self-service areas.

While on the subject of statistics, I mentioned earlier the many nationalities on board. This was the breakdown: American

982, British 691, Canadian 344, Russian 158, Australian 136, Mexican 36, Dutch 37, Spanish 27, German 27. There were 41 nationalities in all, though in the case of some countries they only boasted one representative.

Time to pack our cases, which would be collected that night. Tomorrow we would dock in Xingang. Since leaving Laem Chabang we had travelled 5273 miles. It had been a great trip. Perhaps it would have been better if the ship had been smaller, especially when everyone was disembarking, but it was a beautiful vessel and in spite of the number of people on board it never seemed crowded and it was always possible to find a quiet space.

We left the ship at about 9am. Getting everyone on to the coaches was somewhat chaotic. Our coach driver, who spoke no English, was presented a list of names of passengers who were supposed to be on his bus. There was no way he could have pronounced them and I ended up doing the roll call. Eventually we did get away from the port.

Although the cruise was finished, the holiday was not. We were bound for Beijing.

It was a rather misty morning and when we arrived two and a half hours later, it had still not cleared. The landscape was featureless. It was flat with lots of canals and pools. We reckoned that much of it may have been swamp land that had been cleared. Everywhere was very dry and dusty. A feature of that time of the year is that they get dust blowing down from Siberia.

Our hotel in Beijing was the Novotel. It was right in the centre of the city – opposite MacDonald's! While our passports were being sorted out, a somewhat lengthy process, we thought a snack from the buffet would be a good idea. Unfortunately, it was up a staircase with no other means of access. Not to worry – I brought the food down to the reception area and we ate there.

No time to waste. Several trips were included in our stay in Beijing and that afternoon we were to visit the Temple of Heaven. This was where the emperors of the Ming and Quing dynasties held their ceremonies for praying to heaven for good harvests. It was first built in 1420 and was continually reconstructed and enlarged from that time. In 1918 the site was opened as a public park. There were many buildings on the site: the Hall of Prayer, the Dragon Pavilion, the Imperial Vault of Heaven, the Circular Mount Altar and several others. It was very hard going with cobblestones and flights of steps. The buildings were generally inaccessible. What we had been told about not touring China with a wheelchair was certainly true as far as the Temple of Heaven was concerned. With assistance, we managed to get from one side to the other. I went up to the top of he Circular Mount Altar. There was a special place there for praying and there was a group of Chinese schoolchildren taking turns to stand on it.

The bar in the hotel was also up a flight of stairs. Employees who were happy to help carried Noel up. There was a very good art exhibition in the bar and the young woman who was the organiser took us round and told us about the various works. Some of them were very good.

The hotel had several restaurants that were accessible by lift. We settled for the Chinese one that evening. The food was very different to what we had eaten before in the West and was accompanied by jasmine tea throughout the meal.

Our room was very satisfactory and we went to bed that night looking forward to the Great Wall the following day.

We were up at 6am ready for an 8am start after breakfast. It was more than two hours from Beijing.

We expected that the coach would drive there direct, but no: commercial break; we were going to visit a place that specialised in jade. No complaints though, the work there was excellent. With the aid of a bit of bargaining we bought a picture for ourselves. Noel was given a piece of lucky jade, which he still wears on a chain round his neck.

Beijing weather can be very dodgy and cold at that time of the year (15th November) but we were so lucky. It was a beautifully clear and sunny day and the temperature was not so low.

Noel got annoyed with me because I said he would not be able to go up on to the wall. There were several flights of steps. He was determined that he would, and with the help of our driver and guide and a Chinese policeman, he was carried up. I left him there while I walked up to the next fort.

The Great Wall covers 7,300km in total. They reckon that it is one of the few features on earth that can be seen from outer space. The section we visited, the Badaling Great Wall, was first built in 290BC. The existing one was rebuilt by the Ming Dynasty more than 600 years ago. It is 1,000m above sea level. The height of the wall averages 7.8m and the top averages 5.8m. As you walk up you can see it snaking across the mountains. The countryside around is wild mountain scenery. There were a lot of people walking up, but that in no way diminished its splendour.

When I got back to where I had left Noel he was not there. How do you explain to people that you have lost your husband on the Great Wall? After looking around I found him down below. His kind helpers had lifted him down the steps again.

Before we went to China, Noel had announced that he intended to buy our two sons those traditional fur hats. No way could I convince him that they would probably never wear them. We duly purchased two that day to add to our Christmas present collection.

Our grandsons said they had photographed their dad wearing his in bed on Christmas morning but to my knowledge neither have worn them since. But when Noel makes his mind up, that's it.

We lunched that day at a Friendship Store. They are all over China and sell all manner of traditional goods. It was a very good lunch. Chinese food with a difference again.

We bought a mahjong set for Roland's birthday. It weighed a ton.

Our next stop was the Sacred Way, lined with some very good sculptures. At the end of it was the Ming Emperor's mausoleum.

Our drive into Beijing was during the evening rush hour. The roads are huge to cope with the traffic levels and there are special lanes for the millions of cyclists. It was getting dark but none of the bicycles had lights on them. The city was very colourful with lots of neon advertising signs and one of the main roads had strings of lights across, which looked like a mesh of gold in the distance.

The Beijing road system is really impressive. In the city they have many lanes and there are numerous expressways and multi level intersections. There are five ring roads round the city and they were building a sixth one.

One of the restaurants in the hotel was French, complete with announcements for the arrival of Beaujolais Nouveau. So we decided to eat French that evening. It had been a good day and we were impressed with everything we had seen.

There was an organised trip the following day to the Forbidden City. After the Temple of Heaven, we decided to give it a miss as it promised to be equally difficult. Also, we rather fancied a day in Beijing doing what we wanted.

It is important to realise that in China most people do not speak English, and certainly not taxi drivers. Hotels give you little cards with the names of places you may wish to visit printed in Chinese, but we neglected to get one.

We walked to Tiananmen Square. I knew it was big enough to hold a million people – the entire population of Birmingham. It is absolutely vast. It was a Saturday morning and there were masses of Chinese visitors, but there was still loads of space. There were long queues to visit the Memorial Hall and another building that had a big picture of Chairman Mao on the front, but we had no intention of visiting either of these.

We just walked around taking in the atmosphere. There were many big statues and lots of policemen standing on little red pedestals. When you see Chinese families around it is noticeable that they only have one child and you get the impression by their attitude that their only child is very precious.

It was another sunny morning and we walked a long way before we decided to take a taxi. The taxis in Beijing were not very large and we drove along with the wheelchair sticking out of the boot. We wanted to go to Silk Street Market but we could not make the driver understand. He took us on a long drive, which was actually very interesting because we saw a lot of the city, and we eventually ended up at a large shopping centre. Having got there, we decided to leave the taxi and have a look around. It was called Shopping City and the main unit in it was a large department store. The fashion department had a wide range of designer clothes – genuine, not copies. It was not a tourist place and the customers were nearly all well-to-do Chinese. We encountered a European man there who gave us a little card with those Chinese words for places to go. Perhaps we would get to Silk Street Market after all. Armed with our card, we hailed another cab and reached our desired destination. Silk Street Market is housed on six or seven floors. Hundreds of traders each have a small section. Here is where you will get your fake Prada bags and Rolex watches and you can bargain for them. With a lift to all the floors it was easily accessible and we used the opportunity to buy the last few items for our Christmas gift list and an extra in-flight bag (Prada, of course) because our luggage had expanded somewhat.

Another cab back to the hotel and time to relax with a coffee before our evening outing to sample that famous speciality, Peking roast duck. When we got to the restaurant, there was another staircase but Noel was getting quite used to being carried up. We were with a group, which was just as well as it lacked any other customers. The duck was good. The Great Wall wine would not have gone down too well in Bordeaux.

Sunday 27th November – time to leave the Far East and fly back to England. We had really enjoyed our trip but it wasn't over yet. We left the hotel at 9.30. It was only a 25-minute journey to Beijing airport along one of the many expressways. Arriving there we were fast-tracked as usual through the formalities of checking in, including filling in forms. Other passengers were not so lucky. There were long queues and they were moving rather slowly. We were placed next to each other on the plane but many couples were not. It seemed that they were going to have to improve their efficiency at the airport. We were on a British Airways 777, which was not as comfortable as the jumbo that took us to Bangkok. There was definitely less legroom and neither of us is very tall.

The flight was proceeding routinely when there was an announcement "Is there a midwife on board". I had noticed a young woman who was pregnant earlier and it would seem that she had probably gone into early labour. There was a midwife on board and a doctor. A short time later there was another announcement "We have a medical emergency and are going to land". And land we did – in the middle of Siberia surrounded by ice and snow. The airport was called Syktvar and I don't think it was in the habit of welcoming 777s. The young woman was taken off the plane to a local hospital and subsequently returned to the plane. Refuelling was necessary and I think there was some discussion about who was going to pay for that! In the intense cold, the plane had iced up and de-icing had to take place. We were there for three and a half hours before being airborne again.

Some time later, another announcement. The captain told us he had bad news. The crew had exceeded their flying time. They had applied for special permission to carry on to Heathrow but this had been refused. We were going to land at Stockholm to wait for another crew to be flown out. This time we left the plane and were greeted by fruit juice and sandwiches in a deserted Stockholm airport. Another two hours delay.

We eventually reached Heathrow at 2.30am, eleven hours late, with our pregnant passenger still on board. Noel's wheelchair had to be collected from the carousel where we discovered that they had managed to seriously damage one of the brakes. At that hour there was no one to report it to.

We were given a free stay at the Hilton hotel for the remainder of the night. It is just a short walk through a tunnel from Terminal 4. We had a nice room and a good breakfast. I went back to the terminal to report the damage and was told I should phone or email. I had no time to follow it up as Isobel, our daughter-in-law, was collecting us. We went back to their house in Surrey. I had put all our Christmas shopping in one case so that we could leave it in England, as we would be returning in a couple of weeks. In the meantime, it was off to Gatwick and in the air again to Alicante. That plane was half empty. Our car was conveniently parked ready for us at the airport. Soon we were back home at the end of an immensely enjoyable trip.

Chapter 11

All About Scooters

About three years after his stroke and having been confined to a wheelchair for outdoor activities, Noel started to get interested in the idea of having an electric scooter. Disability scooters have advanced considerably in both availability and design over the years. At that time, we were living in Spain and they were not readily available. We saw an advertisement in our local English paper for an agent in Malaga. We lived on the Costa Blanca, but he did visit our area and brought one along for Noel to try. We bought it, along with more independence for him. He could not use it directly from our house, as our road was not made-up and had an appalling surface, but it was the type that would fit into the boot of a car.

With the idea of accommodating a scooter, we had recently bought a larger car after our previous one packed up. The boot of our Renault Scenic was adequate and we had room to carry a wheelchair as well in the back of the car. You may wonder why we needed to have room for both. Electric scooters are brilliant on flat surfaces and can tackle quite steep hill, but they cannot mount a pavement that is more than a few inches. If the restaurant where you want to eat has one or two steps – or even more – there are usually people on hand to offer assistance and carry the wheelchair and occupant up. You cannot carry a scooter up anywhere. So although they offer freedom, that freedom is, necessarily, limited.

We had two local towns. Calpe was fine, especially along the promenades by the sea. Even in the town there were ramps on many of the roads. I would say, in passing, that the people who design and construct ramps have probably never had to use one. If they did they would realise the shortcomings. Some shops and restaurants put them in to conform with the law of disabled access, and you would need to be suicidal to attempt to use them. Our other local town, Benissa, was totally impossible for a scooter. The kerbs are high and there are no road crossings with proper ramps. The moral is: know your place. If you are going somewhere you haven't been before, play safe, and make sure you have a wheelchair.

I worked in a charity shop in Moraira every Thursday morning. Moraira is a small town on the coast. Most of it is flat and it is very well provided with ramps. While I was at work, Noel used to spend his morning going round exploring and chatting to people who got to know him and his scooter. Moraira has a marina and Noel likes boats so he often went down there and to the fishing port.

I was working one week when a Spaniard came into the shop to inform me that he had rescued my husband from the marina. My first response was "What has he got up to now". I was assured that he was okay. I accompanied my informer down to the marina, and there was Noel sitting on the pavement dripping wet! I never really got to the bottom of how it happened – I suspect a three-point turn at the end of those wooden decking walkways that go between the boats (which only boat owners are supposed to use!). The result had been to launch himself on his scooter into the water. He could very easily have drowned. He only has the use of one arm and leg and was never a brilliant swimmer anyway. Somehow he had managed to hold on to a rope. Two Germans nearby had spotted him and alerted the Spanish man and his friend who were in a small boat. They had hauled him out of the water and come to inform me. There was no sign of the scooter. It was at the bottom of the harbour and one of them put on his diving gear to bring it up. That was how deep the water was that Noel had fallen into. Surprisingly he wasn't too fazed by it. I went back to the shop and grabbed some dry clothes then got him and the scooter into our car. The scooter was not happy about the incident. In fact, it was so unhappy that it never went again. I dried it out but batteries do not like salt water.

The story of Noel falling into the marina has been one of those that our acquaintances have been dining out on ever since. He was greeted with offers of wetsuits and asked if he had left his flippers outside the restaurant. He was lucky though.

We had not been able to get insurance for the scooter in Spain so it looked like it was a write-off. When we went back to England that summer I took it with us and phoned the manufacturers. A very helpful manager there supplied us with the parts that would have to be replaced at a reasonable price and Noel was mobile once more with instructions never to go near the water again!

English towns are generally disability friendly. When we returned to the UK for holidays, our local town is Horsham in Sussex. Like many others, it has a Shopmobility scheme where disabled people can hire electric scooters at a special office in the main car park. All the shops have flat access. Noel has complete independence on his own vehicle here, which is a joy. The only situation that is even easier is a modern indoor shopping centre where shops don't even have doors and there are lifts to all levels. Fortunately these exist in most parts of the world these days.

Noel kept that scooter for some time but by now other models were coming on the market and he eventually got a new one. It did not take very long for him to realise that he had made a mistake. It was a three-wheel version with only one wheel at the front and not very stable. After it had tipped over a few times with him on it – usually when I was not around and he had to be rescued and put back on again – he decided on a part-exchange for a four-wheel version. This time we made sure that it was insured. We didn't really think anything would happen to it, but with Noel's scooter history so far, you never know.

One day we went to a meeting in a restaurant very close to where we live. By now our road was asphalt so he could use his scooter from our home. After lunch, trying to get back up a rather steep hill, it started to play up. Two friends were coming to see us, so we got Noel into their car and parked the vehicle at the side of the road. I took the key, without which no one could start it, and went home with them in the car. A very short time later, I went back in our car to collect it. I stared at where we had left it in disbelief. It wasn't there. Somebody had stolen it.

Fortunately, we were able to claim on insurance this time. We had to visit the local *guardia* to get a statement. This was in Spanish, our insurers were English, and when I got the confirmation that they would pay us to buy another one, the voice was obviously Indian. I had a mental picture of an Indian trying to decipher a Spanish *denuncia*. Armed with our insurance money, we purchased yet another one. The mobility market is one which has expanded tremendously since we got our first one. His new one was the best yet.

Unfortunately, his one hand has deteriorated and he now finds it impossible to manipulate his scooter but really wants to maintain his independence. He felt that a powerchair would be the solution as the control lever is much lighter and is situated on the arm. We purchased a GoChair, which has proved to be a great success.

Chapter 12

Vive La France

After living in Spain for 11 years, Noel began to think that he would like a change of location. For some reason he got a fixed idea about Lot et Garonne in southwest France. He even started looking in property magazines to find out what the prices were in the area. He insisted that I contact an estate agent to obtain some details. I can't pretend that I really shared this enthusiasm, but when we travelled through France in the summer 2005 en route from England to Spain we agreed that we would spend a few days exploring the area. We used the agents in Nerac as a starting point and through them viewed several properties. One of them was delightful but totally impractical – far too large for us. The price was good, or it would have been if we had had any money to spare. Until we sold our Spanish home, there was no way that we could consider buying anything.

We spent several days based in the Campanile in Agen. I agreed that it was a charming part of the country but was not at all sure that I wanted to leave Spain for France.

However, as far as Noel was concerned, the idea was not going to go away. I was adamant that I did not want to buy a house in France though I did not mind spending time there. Our part of Spain was getting steadily more developed. The moral seemed to be: if there's a space, fill it – often with large high-rise. We had owned our villa for 25 years. Perhaps it was time for a change. I also wanted to spend more time in England and see our family more frequently.

It was in the magazine French Property News that we found a compromise – a static mobile home for sale in Lot et Garonne. It was a bit further north than Nerac but we agreed we would have a look at it. We had no idea whether a mobile home would be any use for someone disabled like Noel but there was only one way to find out.

So one rather cold February day we set off to investigate. We left our Spanish home early in the dark and we arrived at Levignac de Guyenne in the dark about ten hours later. It was the sort of journey we had done often but not usually in the middle of winter. Max and Sara, who run Parc St Vincent, had allocated a chalet for our use, as the mobile home we wanted to view was full of the owner's belongings. Sara told us that there was a restaurant in a neighbouring town but it was further than we anticipated, the roads were deserted and very dark, so we ended up eating cornflakes for our dinner. My enthusiasm for a French home was not flourishing. In fact, I would say it was diminishing rapidly. But in the morning the sun was shining and the world always looks better when the sun shines. We had a look at the mobile home. Unlike most newer models, it did not consist solely of fixed units. The lounge was quite spacious and nicely furnished courtesy of Ikea. The bedroom had a double bed and lots of storage space. The kitchen was better than mine in Spain. The bathroom had a shower but it was over the bath. No good for Noel but conversion looked possible. It had a large area of decking outside and central heating inside. We had our own parking area right in front, which meant I could park very close to the front door. There were three steps with a rail and we worked out how to get Noel in. So we made a decision on the spot. Yes, we would buy it. There was no need to stay any longer so we set off back to Spain.

The price was very reasonable, the owners lived in England, an endowment policy of mine had just matured and in a few weeks the deal was completed. Noel had got what was very like a cosy little bungalow in France for a fraction of the price of a house and I was very happy with the outcome.

At Easter we went there for a short holiday. Our daughter, her partner and our granddaughter came out from England for a week. They stayed in the chalet where we had spent that first night. Next door but one to us, it was just like they were neighbours. Our new French home was proving enjoyably successful.

Three homes were really one too many. So we put our Spanish villa up for sale, thus starting what was to become a somewhat lengthy saga. That summer we returned to Levignac and were really able to explore the area. We always carry Noel's scooter in the boot and his wheelchair in the back of the car. One thing we did discover quite quickly was that scooter use would be limited. France is not so disabled-friendly as England. Many towns and villages are old. They have high kerbs and often cobblestones. That is why it is so important to have manual transport. An ordinary wheelchair with a pusher can overcome most problems, though hacking up hills can be a bit exhausting. But I suppose it's good for your heart rate!! The hypermarkets were brilliant and Noel and his scooter were objects of interest. In our local English town there are people on scooters buzzing around all over the place. We seldom saw one in France and not that many people in wheelchairs. There must be disabled people – do they not go out? As we got to know the local towns better, we began to find ways where he could get around, though some remained wheelchair only.

Lot et Garonne is a scenic area. It is agricultural with hectares of sunflowers and maize. There are huge vineyards and many chateaux to visit and sample the wines. There are roads bordered by long straight lines of trees, which is so typically French. The rivers are wide and beautiful. The summers are hot, punctuated regularly by very dramatic thunderstorms. The weekly markets in all the towns sell wonderful fresh produce. We particularly enjoyed the evening markets they have in the summer season. Our local village, Levignac de Guyenne, had one every Friday. As well as selling local produce, it is a wonderful opportunity for social eating and drinking. Rows of tables are laid out, food and

144

wine or beer can be purchased, and everyone just sits together chatting. A really good opportunity to practice some French and for many of the locals to have a go at their English.

Now we have our cosy little home there, we intend to visit France very regularly and explore many more areas of this fascinating country.

Chapter 13

A Year of Mixed Fortunes

The year 2007 was a year of mixed fortunes. It got off to a very good start. After spending Christmas in England, we went to France via Eurotunnel from Folkestone to Calais. That must be the perfect travel option for the disabled passenger. You drive the car on to a special train and just sit there in your vehicle for about 30 minutes. At the other end you drive off again. The motorway is only a short distance and then you are away through France. Noel had bought me a satnav for my birthday. Perhaps it would solve our navigation problems. Like most couples we do not agree on the best route to take, and when we get lost it is always the other person's fault! Now I could argue with 'Jane', our satnav navigator, rather than Noel – and I have to admit there are times when I do.

We had planned to stay at two Campaniles in Orleans and Perpignon en route to Spain. I always ring and make a booking in advance to ensure that we get a suitable room on the ground floor. They are inexpensive and have quite good restaurants.

Our journey went smoothly and the satnav guided us well. It was especially good going round the Paris ring road. We spent two pleasant nights at the hotels and on the Friday morning we were but a short distance from Spain when disaster struck. Approaching the *peage* to join the motorway at Perpignan, the side of our car was hit by an extremely large truck. Neither of us was injured in any way but it is not nice to see bits of your car all over the road. There was no way we could drive any further. The driver of the truck was Czech. He did not speak English, French or Spanish. The only word he seemed to know was *polizia* but it was the morning rush hour and they never came. We are members of RACE (the automobile association of Spain) and their response to my phone call was brilliant. The Czech driver and I managed to complete a damage form between us and then Noel and I went on a new type of travelling. We always refer to rescue vehicles by the Spanish word *grua* because somehow to me it is descriptive of what they do. We sat aloft in our car and with a journey of about 600km to our home, I thought I could really enjoy this mode of transport down the motorway.

But that was not to be. We were taken to a garage in Perpignan. We spent the morning there and had lunch in the café opposite. When a taxi arrived to take us to Girona, we loaded in some of our belongings but had to leave Noel's scooter behind in the boot of our car. We were now on the way to Spain. The taxi took us to a car hire company where RACE had arranged an Opel Zafiro for us. Soon we were on the motorway and eventually reached Benissa at ten o'clock at night. It had been a long day but at least we were unharmed and we were home again.

A week later another *grua* brought our car to a local garage. We were worried that it might be considered a write-off but the insurance company gave the go ahead for repairs. It was at the garage for two months. We hired a car for one week but after that decided we would manage without. We had a local supermarket and Noel and his scooter became extremely useful for carrying shopping. For people who usually went out and about quite a lot, being at home so much was an unusual experience and one that we found rather relaxing.

Our house in Spain was on the market but, although people came to look, no one had made an offer. In the summer we left for France to spend some time in our mobile home.

Exploring with a satnav provided entertainment. We would decide on a place to visit and let it take us there. Sometimes we would choose a location which proved to be very difficult with a wheelchair – steep hills and those deadly cobblestones – but Noel always enjoyed drives through lovely scenery.

August 24th was his 80th birthday. The plan was that all our family would come to France for the week. Our eldest son had booked a suitable property near St Foy la Grande, not far from us. Suitable, except for one major disadvantage. Bedrooms, all six of them, with bathrooms, were on the ground floor, but the living accommodation was on the floor above at the top of a stone staircase. We discussed this in advance and decided to go ahead. Our younger son, Roland, is very strong and has frequently got Noel and wheelchair up flights of stairs and was confident that he could do so again. There were 11 of us. The house was an old chai (a vineyard building) that had been fantastically renovated. It had lovely views over surrounding vineyards and woodland. The accommodation was luxurious and spacious. We all had a wonderful week and Roland did a sterling job with Noel, wheelchair and staircase.

We returned to our somewhat smaller French home only to receive a call from our agent in Spain that he had a buyer for our villa who wanted to complete very quickly.

The next day we were on the road south again. That week we organised all the belongings that we wanted to take to either France or England, paid several visits to the charity shop where I used to work and several more to the local skip. The removal company collected our stuff and then our buyer had problems with his mortgage and could not complete. Fortunately, we were selling the house with all the contents we did not want, so we still had a bed, table and chairs and TV. We camped out there for several more weeks and nothing had materialised. Power of attorney was organised with our fiscal agents. We had to be back in England in mid-October so off we went again, spending a week in France on the way.

Why did we have to be back in England in mid-October? The 26th was the date of our Golden Wedding and a celebration was organised. We had a lunchtime party at The Tin Drum in Brighton. We do have a wonderful family and again they did us proud. It was also an opportunity to meet up with many friends from all phases of the past 50 years.

But the events of 2007 were not quite over yet. Being married for 50 years is a good reason for celebration and there is still a lot of the world out there to explore. We had always said we would visit South America and on November 9th we set off from Heathrow.

Chapter 14

Sailing Down to Rio

We had decided that we would have a holiday to celebrate our Golden Wedding back in April. Both of us fancied a trip to South America. Noel's mobility is not as good as it used to be and travelling overland was not really an option as it involves much getting on and off coaches. A cruise seemed the solution and we knew from experience that our previous voyages had proved very successful. I trawled the internet for the options available. There were many. Which countries did we want to visit? Should we go for Brazil, Chile, and Argentina? How much did we want to spend? Saga had an interesting one that went down the Amazon but it was a bit above our budget. We have never worried too much about the cruise line; the destinations are the important thing.

Eventually we settled on a trip across the Caribbean to several locations in Brazil, the potential highlight being two days in Rio de Janeiro. Azamara cruises were a new part of the Celebrity group. We were told that the *Azamara Journey* was a new vessel. This was not strictly true – it was a revamped older vessel. Had we known this we may have made a different choice. But more about that later. We also enquired into the possibility of Noel travelling with his scooter rather than the wheelchair, provided that the ship were able to provide us with a wheelchair which we could use when going out on trips in the ports. They said they could not guarantee that there would be one available, which again was not strictly true. However, we decided that it would be a safer option all round to travel with Noel's wheelchair as we had always done in the past.

On November 10th 2007 Barry, our local taxi driver, picked us up at 5.45 in the morning bound for Terminal 3, Heathrow. Being Saturday, the traffic was light and we arrived with plenty of time in hand. As usual, we had our one large case, which I could pull along with my left hand while steering the wheelchair with my right. There was no need to indulge in our customary queue jumping; we were just directed straight to the first-class check-in.

Our flight to Miami took off at 9.45am. We had been allocated good seats in the central section close to the toilet. The journey was totally uneventful and the food reasonably good. What more could one ask for.

It took about one and a half hours to clear immigration and collect our baggage at Miami airport. We were booked into the Wyndham hotel nearby for the night. The hotel sent along a disabled vehicle, which made the transfer easy.

Once again we had one of those enormous bedrooms, which seem to be the norm in most US hotels. It was still only mid-afternoon, though our day had been going on for quite a long time. We sat on a sunny terrace drinking Budweiser at twelve dollars a bottle.

Americans certainly pay a lot for their drinks but the rate of exchange at that time was two dollars to the pound. Financially it was good for us Brits.

We had a really good night's sleep and to our surprise did not wake up at the crack of dawn. There was nothing to visit near the hotel so we had an excellent leisurely breakfast and spent the morning sitting around in the sunshine. The terrace overlooked a park with a river and a golf course.

A coach picked us up about midday to transfer to the ship. Noel managed to get up the steps with my help – but it was not easy.

The *Azamara Journey* is a smaller vessel than those we had holidayed on previously, and as we explored it we realised that it was not the modern ship we had been led to believe. It had the same sort of bumps to negotiate that we had experienced on our first trip on the *Emerald* some years ago. They occurred every time we went through a door from one section of the boat to another and there were very heavy doors, which had to be held open for us. Fortunately, as ever, members of the crew and other passengers were only too ready to assist, but there were times when I had to go looking for them.

Our stateroom was very good (they don't call them cabins any more) and our steward was known as a 'butler'. He even got dressed up in a tailcoat in the evenings. Talk about pseudo snobbery, but they were trying to sell the Azamara line as a luxury item!

It was interesting leaving the port of Miami. There were six cruise vessels lined up as well as ours. Hopefully they were not all going to the same destinations. The container port was enormous.

Another feature of the *Azamara* was not having to dress up in the evenings, no formal dinners and no fixed seating for dining. This suited us very well. You just asked to share a table and had the pleasure of chatting to all sorts of different people. The majority of passengers were Americans but there were also many Canadians and quite a number of Brits. No complaints about the food. As usual, it was excellent. Dinner offered a selection of starters, soups, salads, main courses and desserts. Every day there was a different menu. No way could either of us manage five courses but the leisurely pace of the meals was great. Some of the desserts were to die for, especially if you happened to be a chocoholic!

We continue to be astonished at the number of cruises some people have done. One couple who dined with us on the first evening had been on 33 and that certainly was not the highest total we encountered. Americans particularly seem to go on several a year. On our fourth, we really were novices.

On the Monday we had a day at sea. This was a chance to find our way around the ship and to discover what was going on. There were plenty of activities but I have to confess that we were not enthusiastic participants. We would go to lectures if the subject appealed, but we are not really into a lot of games and quizzes and we do not play bridge. One of the features of this particular cruise was a number of days at sea and I was a bit doubtful about that. I will happily swim but the pool on the *Azamara* was not very large and many rather large American women had a tendency to stand in the middle and chat, making it necessary to try and negotiate the water around them. We went to the first show of the trip in the evening. The resident group were young and talented – three Americans and a girl from England.

We had looked at all the tours offered by the ship at the various ports of call and realised that many were quite unsuitable for Noel, often because they involved walking over cobblestone streets or pathways through the forests. However, at our first destination, Turks and Cacos, I really wanted to go snorkelling as the coral reef there is considered to be of world class. Noel would have to stay on the boat. We duly went down to the quay to board and the snorkelling instructors got him on without any difficulty. As mentioned before, Noel could use a camera with a special device attached to his wheelchair, which had previously proved very successful, so he was able to take photographs of my snorkelling exploits. The snag was that in his wheelchair he was unable to move around to focus the camera on me in the water. I am not the most proficient snorkeller on earth and it turned out he was not the most proficient photographer – because none of them were much good.

Our next destination was a bay where we were going to share the sea with stingrays. The boat sounded a special signal and they all started to arrive. It may have been in the open sea but these fish had been trained to respond, knowing that they would get a good feast. The water wasn't very deep. We didn't have to swim – it was possible to walk around. I was amazed at the size of the stingrays and how friendly they were. Certainly a very interesting experience.

Grand Turk is a very small island. We took a taxi to Cockburn Town, which is the capital, and went for a walk around. There was a lovely little Anglican church, St Mary's, that was beautifully maintained. It had been established in 1879. It may have been the main town on the island but it was little more than a village by the beach. It had a quiet charm. A lovely friendly female taxi driver took us back to the port. The island may be small but the port area was ultra smart and modern, built only a year before by Carnival Cruises. It had a shopping centre and several restaurants and bars. Time to relax and try the local beer. Well, nearly local – Jamaican Red Stripe and very good too.

The next day was at sea. Noel went to a talk about cricket, something of a mystery to the Americans on the ship. I see enough of it on TV, so I took part, not very successfully, in a table tennis tournament. I actually love playing table tennis but never get enough opportunities to practice.

The cricket lecturer was Richard Cowley, an Englishman who had lived in Uruguay and been involved in many activities there, including the Cultural Attaché at the British Embassy in Montevideo. He was a very entertaining speaker, and in the course of our trip he gave a series of talks about South America, which provided a fascinating insight into various aspects of the continent.

During the day, when having afternoon tea, we first encountered Fabian, a Brazilian who was going to be very helpful to us later in the trip.

On Thursday we arrived in Dominica. We docked at Cabrits at about 9am. Apparently, most of the bigger cruise vessels go to the capital, Roseau, so we had the port all to ourselves. None of the tours offered by the *Azamara* seemed really suitable for Noel, so we joined up with four other passengers and hired a taxi. There are always plenty of taxis for hire at all the ports and are definitely our best option. The drivers offer tours, often very similar to those available on the ships, and usually for a fraction of the price.

Dominica is a hilly, volcanic island with untouched tropical rainforests. It is 15 miles wide and 29 miles long. Apparently it has 364 rivers and 200 waterfalls; this seems pretty incredible. We went to the Emerald Pool, which featured one of the waterfalls. To reach it involved a walk through the rain forest. Definitely not a wheelchair activity and Noel had to stay at the top. It was a steep descent with several flights of steps. There were a lot of people, but I came back a different route and had the forest all to myself. It was lovely. The journey from the port took about an hour each way so we saw much of the island. It was lunchtime as we drove though a small town and once more in the Caribbean I was impressed by how smart all the children looked in their school uniforms.

Time to stop at a beach bar and to sample some more of the local beer. Our younger son, very much a world traveller, collects beer bottles from all his locations and we sometimes take back empty ones in our luggage to add to his collection.

Our last call in the Caribbean was Barbados. As we had been there before, when we had gone on that jeep safari through the sugar plantations to the northern side of the island, we decided we would just visit the capital, Bridgetown. It was pouring with rain that morning but we managed to get a cab quite quickly and spent our time dashing in and out of shops until it eased off. Supposedly duty-free, many of the shops cater very much for tourists. It is not an easy place to push a wheelchair. The pavements are not smooth and the kerbs high but we had a good wander around.

When we got into the taxi to return to the ship, our driver had his radio tuned to one of those American religious programmes. It was truly awful but he was more than enthusiastic joining in with alleluias, amens and hand clapping as he drove along!

We were now scheduled for four days at sea as we sailed to the coast of Brazil. Other passengers told us that the sea had been rough during the night and that they had found it difficult to sleep. Our stateroom was on Deck 3, very low down in the ship, so we were not affected at all. There are only a very limited number of staterooms with disabled facilities on any cruise vessel, so there is not much choice of location. They are always placed at the end of corridors near to the lifts, which is an advantage. When the ship rolls, it causes the water in the swimming pool to slosh back and forth. That day they had to close the pool because it was coming right over the edges.

Spending several days and consequently moving around the ship a lot for different activities involved crossing many bumpy thresholds. These began to take their toll on the wheelchair and one of the front wheels became rather wobbly. A member of the maintenance staff offered to try and repair it. I then discovered that there were, in fact, many wheelchairs on the ship, all lined up under the staircase on Deck 4, and that the original information that there may not be one available to borrow was very definitely incorrect. Noel's was strengthened though it was not possible to put it completely right. After that, we often used those available and even took them ashore for some trips. However, they were a bit wider with large wheels at the sides. It made us realise that our compact carer chair was indeed the most practical for travelling around in taxis etc.

Afternoon teas were a most civilised occasion. A choice of beverages like Earl Grey, scones with jam and cream, a selection of pastries, all consumed to the accompaniment of soft music from a resident harpist (who was incidentally the wife of the man in charge of the computer facilities). It was on the Sunday, at afternoon tea, that we met up with Fabian and Marcos again. They both worked for H Stern, a big international jewellers who have their head office in Rio. We had been told by the tour organisers on the ship that their trips in Rio would not be suitable for someone in a wheelchair. They seemed doubtful that he would be able to go to the top of either Sugar Loaf or Corcovado, the mountain that has the giant statue of Christ at the top. Needless to say, we were not happy about this. We had chosen this trip with Rio as the highlight and were determined that we would not miss out. Fabian and Marcos came from the city and we discussed this with them. They said they would sort out a trip for us. At this stage we had no idea what they had in mind but it sounded interesting.

Through the lecturer Richard Cowley, we were learning much about the history of the Portuguese and the British in Brazil and about the traditional music and dance. He was a very entertaining speaker.

At 11 pm on Monday 19th November, we crossed the equator and celebrated with a glass of champagne. The following day in the afternoon there was a fun ceremony about the crossing. Crew members were dressed up as King Neptune, as mermaids, as pirates. It culminated in the captain having to 'walk the plank' when he was thrown into the swimming pool. The captain of the *Azamara* was quite young. His wife and his son, three years old, were travelling with him. We have certificates to prove that we are shellbacks (people who have crossed the equator) although we already were, having crossed on one of our previous voyages.

We were scheduled to arrive at Recife in Brazil the following morning, but due to a late departure from Barbados and adverse currents en route, we would not be there until 6pm in the evening. Disappointing but nothing could be done about it. Obviously all trips were cancelled and alternative arrangements had to be made.

There was an opportunity to leave the ship about 6.30pm when a fleet of shuttle buses were laid on to take passengers to a local shopping centre. It was a bit of a scrum but we managed to get Noel and his wheelchair on the bus. It was a good shopping centre – very modern and decked out with tasteful Christmas decorations. Ideal for us to get around. There were several floors served by escalators. The normal lift was out of action but we were shown to another one normally used for goods and were able to go everywhere. Brazilian shops are very stylish. On the top floor were artisans involved in various crafts and we bought our daughter a very unusual lamp. They were created from plastic coca cola bottles with beautiful coloured designs on them.

Back on the ship we had a real treat that evening which had been hastily arranged to compensate for lack of time in Recife. A local troupe of dancers and musicians came on board and gave us a splendid show. They were very talented, performing numerous types of traditional dances in incredible colourful costumes. It was a bit like a mini- carnival. The passengers danced too. It was a jolly evening. It is a regret that Noel cannot dance now – the man who was once declared twist champion of Balham. But I like it and have been known to bop around pushing the wheelchair.

Another day at sea when all the Americans celebrated Thanksgiving, before we arrived at Salvador de Bahia early the next morning. It gets light very early at about 5am, and because we are near the equator, dark a similar time in the evening.

We started our visit there on one of the few excursions we had booked. It was really an orientation trip around the city and once Noel was on the coach he could stay there until the end. As usual we were given the front seats. Salvador is a city of three million inhabitants, 80 percent of whom are of African origin. We toured the modern areas and drove along the beaches but not the old town.

The old town is at the top of a hill overlooking the harbour. It dates from the 16th century and has retained its character. The streets are narrow and cobblestone. Pedestrians reach it via two large lifts up the cliff. Going up in the lift presented no problems but one look at the main square and all the cobbles and we thought, this is not going to be for us. Then we spotted two buggies with drivers who made tours around the town. We were soon in one with the wheelchair in the back. For 25 reales the driver took us everywhere, even the narrowest of streets where no other vehicle could have got through. It was fascinating. The old buildings have been beautifully restored, often in bright colours. Many of them are shops catering for tourists, but selling very interesting ethnic items. There were displays of colourful paintings on wood and traditional Brazilian musical instruments including the *berimbau*, which was for sale everywhere in all sizes.

There are reportedly 300 churches in Salvador. We only saw the outside of several because we were on the buggy. They were architecturally very interesting and I am sure that the interiors were probably lavish and golden but we accepted that with a wheelchair they were not really accessible. However, it was an excellent trip and something we had not expected when we had first emerged from that lift.

Our visit to Salvador finished with a wander around the market before we made our way back to the ship, fortunately within walking distance.

Salvador lies in a bay with 400 islands. It is a lovely setting. Part of the city is a UNESCO heritage site with hundreds of restored buildings. Arriving by ship, we had seen the bay on the coach tour, we had been around the modern city and the beaches, and in the buggy we had experienced the old area. It had, indeed, been a most successful visit to a very interesting and vibrant place.

The following day we arrived in Ilheus, 287 miles south of Salvador. This is the centre of cocoa production and there are many cocoa plantations. However, chatting to a local in the town, he informed us that crops have recently been so affected by a disease that they have to import cocoa to make up the shortfall. In the meantime, efforts are being made to produce a resistant strain.

We took a taxi into what turned out to be an extremely flat and easy town for us to walk around. It was Saturday morning and everyone was out shopping. It was pleasant and not at all touristy. We had been told repeatedly that when going round Rio visitors should remove all their jewellery. I would quite happily relinquish my earrings and put my watch in a pocket but I have two gold chains round my neck that I never ever remove and as I did not intend to do so now, the solution seemed a high-necked t-shirt which would cover them. This became my main purchase in Ilheus. It was obviously a very safe place, so we fixed Noel's camera on his wheelchair and this time he took many very good photographs. There were street vendors selling drinks of coconut milk. They just cracked open the coconut and poured the contents straight into a plastic cup – and it was deliciously refreshing.

Ilheus is famous for its beaches and my underwear that day was a bikini. I really wanted to swim in the sea some time while we were in Brazil. A taxi driver took us out to the beach area. Obviously there was no way Noel and his wheelchair were going to get on those sandy beaches but there were cafes behind. However, it was very quiet there and we were not sure whether we would be able to get a taxi back again later. My Spanish had served me quite well most of the time even though the locals spoke Portuguese, but there didn't seem to be any conversational meeting point between me and this particular taxi driver. So we decided to go back to the ship. I was feeling a bit disappointed and cheated so I went off for a walk from the port to see if I could find a local beach, but no luck. The only one I found was far from clean and sandy.

The following day we were at sea again but it was notable for one thing. I discovered *caipirinha*, the national drink of Brazil. To make it you put sliced lime and sugar in the bottom of the glass and crush them together, add lots of ice and then fill up the glass with Cachaca (which is Brazilian rum). Refreshing and delicious. I was definitely a convert, even if Noel stuck to his red wine!

Fabian and Marcos had left the ship two ports previously. Rumour had it that they had been asked to leave because they were arranging trips for the passengers. These trips would obviously include a visit to H Stern, the jewellers. However, they had told us they would see us port-side when we arrived in Rio and that we would have our own car with a driver and an English-speaking guide who would take us wherever we wanted to go. Sounded too good to be true but we were going along with it.

We docked at Rio early in the morning. After breakfast we left the ship. Sure enough, Fabian was there. We had a car as promised and our guide was Sandro. He was a young Brazilian student who had just started his holidays from school the previous day. It was the first time he had worked for H Stern. He was a delightful lad. It was a rather misty morning but while we had the transport we were determined to see Sugar Loaf and Corcovado.

Sugar Loaf consists of two mountains, the Morro da Urca which is 220m high and the Pao de Acucar, 396m. It got its name because of its distinctive shape and it is visible from all over the city. The descent is in two stages by cable car.

The tour operators on the ship were sceptical that Noel and his wheelchair would get to the top. They were so wrong. The facilities for disabled passengers were excellent. A specially operated little lift took us to the station at the bottom of the cable railway. Staff assisted with entry to the cable cars and when we got to the top it was easy to walk around. The views were fantastic. The clouds were very low but there were sufficient breaks in the mist to see across the city and beyond to the beaches and the sea on both sides. It was a very worthwhile and inspiring experience. Sandro also took on the task of pushing the wheelchair, which gave me a nice break.

At some stage during the day we were to visit the headquarters of H Stern at Ipanema. Noel had decided that he would buy me a ring in Brazil as a memento of our trip and our anniversary, so we were very happy to go there. It was a very impressive establishment and we toured the workshops before making our choice – a double-gold band set with diamonds and emeralds. As I have mentioned before, I am a rock collector, and they had a museum filled with beautiful natural stones and gems. For me, this was the most interesting aspect of the visit.

Ipanema Beach is probably the most famous in the world thanks to the song *The Girl from Ipanema*. It was written by Tom Jobim and Vinicius de Moraes about a real, young and lovely girl who used to go walking there every day and in the 1950s it was a popular hit by Frank Sinatra.

After we had finished the visit to H Stern, we were driven along the road by the beach and I would have loved to be able to say "I swam at Ipanema". It really wasn't a practical idea at that moment and fortunately the sea was quite choppy and therefore not so inviting.

The next beach was Copacabana. They are certainly magnificent – wide and sandy. All along the other side of the road are expensive hotels and apartments. It was time for lunch and Sandos suggested that we should go to a restaurant in Copacabana. We invited him to have lunch with us. There were two sides to the restaurant – meat or fish. We opted for the fish and did we have a great selection of seafood. There was a sumptuous buffet, but in addition to that, the waiter just kept coming to our table with more goodies. The décor was intriguing. There was a wall completely covered with a colourful collection of plates. All manner of interesting objects hung from the ceiling including traditional musical instruments. Full of Brazilian lunchtime diners, it had a great atmosphere.

The weather was not improving but it was now time to visit Christ the Redeemer. We had transport available that day and Sandro to provide assistance if necessary. The next day we would have to do our own thing. Our driver heard on his radio that the forecast for the following day was rain. We all agreed, mist or no mist, we were going for it.

The statue of Christ dominates Rio. It is 38m high, weighs 1145 tons and stands right at the top of Corcovado Mountain. Because of the cloudy conditions, there were not many tourists on the special train, which goes up to the summit. The journey up the mountain was through woodland and there were several stations. We had been told that after leaving the train the access to the final section was by escalator.

This did not sound very wheelchair friendly but to our surprise one of the employees took over and literally propelled Noel and wheelchair up the escalator. He was very proficient and had obviously done it before. So much again for the pessimism of the tour operators on the ship. It was certainly cloudy, but they were drifting. Occasionally there would be a gap and we would see part of the view below. Christ was coming and going. Sometimes the statue was quite clear, sometimes it disappeared altogether but it was quite magical when it appeared as a silhouette in the mist. It is absolutely enormous and tremendously impressive. One can only imagine the task of getting it up to the top of the mountain.

We didn't see a lot of the city below, but we had seen the views from Sugar Loaf in the morning and we felt well rewarded. It had been a most successful day. We had achieved everything we wanted and Sandro had enjoyed his first experience as a tour guide. When we got back to the port I collected my ring from the H Stern outlet there and thanked Fabian. We were so glad we had met him and Marcos.

Noel was tired after the long day out so he retired to bed quite early after dinner. I went on deck to sample some more *caipirinha* and have a few dances. We still had another day in Rio tomorrow.

We wanted to explore downtown so we took a taxi from the port. That took some time, as the traffic was dense and very slow moving. This was an advantage as it gave us plenty of time to look around. We asked the driver to drop us at Centro Cultural at the Banco de Brasilia, as we had been told they had an interesting museum.

It was a beautiful old building with an exhibition of the history and geography of the country. There were lifts and it was all very accessible. They also had an excellent bookshop. Richard Cowley, the lecturer on board the *Azamara*, had given out a list of publications relevant to his various talks. One of these particularly interested Noel, a book called *Flowers of the Amazon Forests* by Margaret Mees. She was an artist who specialised in lovely detailed paintings of plants. They had a copy but we decided not to purchase it then. Our luggage was going to be heavy enough without adding large books. I actually purchased it from Amazon when we got home and gave it to him for Christmas.

We walked through the very busy city centre to the Museo de Bel Artes. We were hoping to see some vibrant Brazilian modern art but that particular art gallery housed a rather strange collection. Many of the paintings were very dark and sombre and we didn't find it very inspiring.

The streets of the city centre were much more vibrant, buzzing with life and people. The weather forecast had been rain, but so far it had held off. When it did start we headed for a restaurant for lunch. It was obviously a place where local office workers went for their midday break. The system was most efficient. As we entered we were given a card. All food was served from a buffet and the cost of the items chosen were punched on the card. When we left we paid the total at a desk. There was not a lot of room between the tables but very helpful staff made room for the wheelchair. I installed Noel with a beer, made my survey of the food available and reported back. There was an excellent selection – meat, fish, pasta and salads, all beautifully presented. And when we paid at the end we were surprised how cheap it was.

It was now turning into a really wet day, so we found the nearest taxi rank and returned to the port. We had really enjoyed our independent tour of the city centre. I was still wearing that high-necked t-shirt. However, the parts of the city we had visited over the two days had been totally unthreatening. It had been reasonably easy to get around with a wheelchair. Two days is only a taster of all that one could see but we had achieved our main objectives and were very happy with the experience.

Our next destination, Paraty, was very different. This was the first time our ship was not going right into port and everyone would be transported on tenders. There was a small fleet of these for the half-hour trip between the ship and Paraty. Noel was always carried in his wheelchair down the ramp from the ship to the shore. On this occasion the carrying continued into the smaller vessel. It was an awkward manoeuvre. I must admit I looked the other way as three strong men got him in, but as usual it was cheerfully achieved. Once on board there was room for him to sit in his wheelchair.

Paraty, which means white fish, is a very old town. Its history dates from 1530 when it was the haunt of pirates and gold seekers. In the 17th and 18th centuries it was the second most important harbour in Brazil, built exclusively for the export of gold to Portugal and was also a centre for the slave trade. Nowadays it is protected by UNESCO and is reckoned to be one of the most beautiful old colonial cities in the world. All around it is the Atlantic rainforest.

We passed numerous islands on our trip in the tender. They were hilly and heavily forested with small buildings visible beside sandy beaches. Scenic and very peaceful.

When we arrived in Paraty we were at the end of a very long pier made up of horizontal wooden slats. The main snag was the gaps between the slats – just the ideal size to trap the small front wheels. I ended up going backwards the whole way so that I was leading with the larger back wheel. Pleasure launches were moored on either side. Nowadays Paraty is a leisure resort for visitors from Rio and Sao Paolo. The whole of the town is paved, if that is the word, with huge cobblestones. A complete no-go. So Noel settled down outside a small café with a beer while I went off to explore. He had his camera set up and took lots of photographs that day.

Paraty has successfully retained its historic atmosphere to the point that I almost felt at times as if I was on a film set. Many of the old houses have been beautifully restored and painted in bright colours. The streets with their cobblestones are narrow and winding. There were many small shops selling a variety of good quality goods – ornaments, clothes, and food. They catered for visitors but they were not tacky. There were local craftsmen. As well as purchasing t-shirts for our granddaughter and myself, I also bought a small bottle of Cachaca so that I could make my favourite Brazilian drink when I got home.

The area is renowned for many beautiful beaches but they were some distance from the town. I pushed Noel along the path by the sea where he took more pictures and I hoped to find a place to swim, but no luck. It was almost the end of our holiday and I was not going to fulfil my ambition of swimming in the south Atlantic. Not to worry – we had achieved many other things. We would be leaving the ship the next day. Time to pack. It was a bit of a squeeze but we got everything into our case. Overnight we sailed to Santos, the port for Sao Paolo.

We left the ship at 9am in the morning. I think it would be fair to describe the departure as somewhat chaotic. It was first time the *Azamara* had made this trip and organisation did leave things to be desired at times. We were transferred from the ship to the port terminal in a very poorly designed disabled vehicle. Our journey to Sao Paolo would be by coach. Noel had great difficulty getting on. If we are left to ourselves and take time we can usually work out a way but when lots of 'helpers' get involved, it can prove much more stressful. Add to that the layout of South American coaches. They have three or four very steep steps and then a narrow entrance into the coach with more steps. We got installed in the front seat ready for the journey.

It was an interesting one over mountains clad in thick rain forest. The road was extremely busy with huge container trucks making their way from the port to the city. We knew that the outskirts of large cities in that part of the world have thousands of people living in shanty towns. We had not been to those areas of Rio but driving into Sao Paolo we could see the very poor conditions of many inhabitants. The shacks were a jumble of timber and corrugated metal. Nearer the city centre were older districts with loads of small businesses. I was struck by the number of small garages – no doubt an indication of the local traffic levels. Downtown was in stark contrast with its gleaming new high-rise office blocks, apartments and hotels. Although we had only viewed it from the windows of a coach, our journey had given us an overview of the largest city in South America and one of the most highly populated in the world.

It was to one of the sleek modern buildings that we were heading – the Hilton Hotel. Arrangements had been made for passengers from the ship to wait there and to leave their luggage in safety. Our flight was leaving early evening but some of the Americans and Canadians would be waiting until much later. Interestingly, we were flying direct to Heathrow but many of them had to make several shorter hops to reach their destination and we would, in fact, reach England before they arrived at their homes. We were warmly welcomed at the hotel with a selection of savoury and sweet canapés and a selection of beverages. It was a very luxurious building surrounded by garden, although it was in the city. Joined to it was a large and very busy shopping mall. It was lunchtime and all the restaurants were crowded, probably with local office workers.

The shops were stylishly Brazilian stocking lots of goods with Christmas in mind. There were some delightful festive decorations but our luggage was already packed and we always keep hand baggage to a minimum. So we settled for some rather original Christmas cards – time for our family to learn Portuguese. Not that we had mastered it much during our trip! The disabled facilities in the centre were excellent. Where there were escalators, a series of shallow ramps had been built at the side. We spent a pleasant hour or so wandering around and it was soon time to depart for the airport. This involved another coach with precipitous steps and Noel had to endure some more manhandling. The airport was fairly quiet. A cup of coffee, a look around a few more shops and it was time to board the BA flight for Heathrow.

We left slightly late but the pilot made up time. Our seats were good and it was uneventful. I would just say that the breakfast was appalling. Flight food is never very exciting but we have experienced a lot over the years and this would have scored 0 out of 10.

We landed at 8am to be greeted by a grey gloomy morning and by our friendly taxi driver Barry, and before long we were home again.

Another successful and enjoyable trip with lots of happy memories. Noel is not as mobile as in the past. He could never walk much but now he can't do it at all. However, walking had not been required. The wheelchair had survived, though I would say to anyone disabled who is planning a cruise, go for a new vessel where the ride around will be much smoother and the doors will open on their own. We had met lots of interesting fellow passengers and as always lots of kind and helpful people both on board and in the places we visited.

We were planning to stay in England for the winter. In the spring we aimed to go to France. After that who knows. There is still a lot of the world out there waiting to be explored.

Chapter 15

Goodbye Spain

We had left Spain in October 2007 with our villa still unsold. The housing market there was disintegrating fast. It was difficult to feel much sympathy for the builders or the estate agents who had been doing very nicely thank you for many years. The ethos seemed to be: if there is a space, fill it – and certainly in our local town Calpe the high-rise was getting higher as the years went by. Now the clients were not coming, prices were falling fast, and the new properties were frequently remaining empty.

Not that this was any consolation to us. No complaints about our agent. He was doing a sterling job showing people round, but there were no offers.

When 2008 arrived, still nobody had come forward with an offer for our Spanish home. We had decided that we were not going back there. Our fiscal agents had power of attorney and our estate agent was still doing his best.

It was the first time we had experienced the winter in the UK for many years but the weather was quite mild and we both enjoyed the pleasure of spending time with our family.

Noel's one useful hand was still deteriorating and he was finding it very difficult to operate the controls for his scooter. However, he wanted the independence and felt that he might be able to manage a powerchair. These are similar to wheelchairs and have a very light lever on the arm, which enables the user to go backwards and forwards. There is a battery underneath. We spent some time investigating the models on the market. It was essential that we had one which that would take apart easily for storage in the boot of our car and was also light enough for me to do so. The answer seemed to be the GoChair by Pride Mobility Products. We arranged a part-exchange with his scooter. It was an instant success. Noel can operate it very efficiently without undue strain to his hand. Much more manoeuvrable than a scooter –you can actually spin it round on the spot. It divides into four parts – back and front of the base, battery and seat – none of them very heavy and taking up a lot less space in the boot than his previous model. I quickly became very adept at assembling it on the pavement.

Spring came and we decided that we would go to France in June. There was a possible buyer for our Spanish property but after all the ups and downs of the past three years we would need some convincing that the sale would actually go ahead. However, with a telephone and a laptop we could negotiate from France as easily as we could from England.

We travelled by our usual route – drive to Portsmouth, take the fastcraft from there to Cherbourg and drive down to Levignac. This can be accomplished in one day. We leave home at 6.15am, board ferry at 8.30 and arrive in France at 11.30 (having put our watches forward one hour). By only making one short stop on the way, we can arrive in the evening. It is just over 400 miles but French motorways are brilliant. Traffic levels are very much lower than the UK and the driving discipline is definitely superior, mainly because drivers return to the inside lane after overtaking.

Noel's mobility had declined since our visit to our mobile home the previous summer and I was a bit concerned whether, even with considerable assistance from me, he would be able to manage the three steps up to the decking and the entrance. When we got there it became obvious that we had a problem. I got Max, who owns Parc St Vincent with his wife Sara, to give us a hand. Within two days Max and his son Robert had built us a splendid wooden ramp and I could push Noel up in his wheelchair. Problem solved.

The sale of our villa went ahead. The emails flew back and forth. We had been forced to drop the price very considerably from when we first started but at least the rate of exchange worked in our favour. A year earlier we would have needed 1.45 euros for every pound sterling – now it was down to 1.26. We really could say goodbye to Spain.

Time to enjoy our holiday in France. We now knew most of the towns and villages around – which ones Noel could use his powerchair and which ones would require me as the wheelchair pusher. About 40 years ago when our family was young we regularly had camping holidays in France. I was interested in pre-history and purchased a book about cave art. Lascaux in the Dordogne is the site of some of the most famous and dramatic examples. We'd decided to choose that area for our holiday. Lascaux, near Montignac, was discovered by two boys out with their dog in 1940. The only evidence of it was a hole in the ground. It was opened to the public in 1948. Unfortunately, by the time we got there, the authorities had closed it again because the breathing of the vast number of visitors was altering the environment and causing damage to the paintings on the walls. So I was out of luck. In 1972 work started on building an exact replica of the main sections. It was completed in 1983.

Now in 2008, it was time for us to visit Montignac again. Caves are not usually accessible to disabled people and this was no exception. However, I achieved my ambition. Lascaux 2, as they call the reconstruction, is fantastic. The paintings of bulls, horses and deer have been reproduced exactly as they were done in the real cave by men who lived 17,000 years ago. All the animals look so alive and the colours glow.

The huge sand dune at Arcachon was also on the list of places we had wanted to visit in the past. Another day trip beckoned. This was not going to be wheelchair friendly but never mind. In fact, Noel sat in a café drinking coffee while I climbed to the top. It is absolutely enormous and getting bigger all the time. It was a lovely sunny day. From the summit the view in one direction was the sparkling sea and the other side were the endless green forests of Landes. Another ambition achieved. The area is

171

famous for seafood, particularly oysters (which we do not like), but we did have an excellent fruits de mer lunch in a restaurant in Arcachon.

We no longer had our house in Spain but we still had a Spanish car. The insurance was due to expire in September and we would have to think about making arrangements in England. Our Scenic had served us very well but it was seven years old and there was a high mileage (albeit in kilometres) plus a bit of a scrape on the side where I had had an argument with an entrance some time previously. Back in England in August, we came to the conclusion that we should consider getting another car. I have mentioned before that a left-hand drive was better for Noel as he could lead with his good leg to get into the passenger seat, but it looked as if he was going to have to adapt to a right-hand drive.

So would I. Obviously for most of my life I had driven an English car but for the past 12 years it had been a continental model. I was used to a left-hand drive in England, now it would be a right-hand drive in France. We bought a four-year-old Scenic and the garage took ours in part exchange. The boot is slightly larger so his powerchair fits easily. There is slightly more space in the back for the wheelchair. Noel has adapted though it is more difficult and he needs more assistance from me, especially bending his right leg, which he cannot do himself.

While we were in France we had our bathroom in England completely remodelled. Out went the bath, which was completely useless for Noel, to be replaced by a wet room. It is brilliant and makes showering so easy. I would say to anyone contemplating doing the same: shop around. All those people who advertise in the disabled sections of Saturday newspapers and magazines are very expensive. The local Social Services recommended a company in the area who specialised in disability conversions. They did a great job at a very good price and we now have really excellent showering facilities. While we were in England we arranged for a plumber in France to replace the bath in our mobile home with a shower, which was also successful. So no excuses now for not being clean and wholesome!

We returned to France in September for another month of lovely sunny weather after England's grey August. Spain now belonged to the past and we were enjoying our dual life between France and the UK.

Chapter 16

Lessons Learned

When I ask Noel what problems he felt he encountered on our travels he would say there was nothing that we could not work out together.

Obviously one has to accept that there are activities and places that are inappropriate for anyone who is disabled in a wheelchair and make one's travel choices accordingly, but as we discovered, many things are possible with the desire to achieve them and a willingness to accept help when necessary.

Wherever we went we found people were always ready to lend a hand. Frequently it was spontaneous. On other occasions we would ask them. Perhaps it is the feeling of 'there for the grace of God go I'. Noel has been carried up many flights of steps and no one has dropped him yet!

We saw an article in a national newspaper a short time ago about disabled travellers. Readers had written in with accounts of bad treatment they had received. We discussed our experiences together and, truthfully, could not come up with a single instance of people being unfriendly or unhelpful.

Whenever family or friends book at a restaurant for us to dine with them, they always enquire about the accessibility of toilets. Many older restaurants in Spain and France particularly tend to locate them in the basement or on the first floor and they are not, therefore, suitable. This is obviously an important issue when travelling. We found that in most modern cities it was not a problem, and there was a wide availability of specially adapted disabled ones. Airports and motorway service areas are always well equipped, though there was one motorway stop in

China when the overflowing squats in the Ladies left much to be desired and I was glad that Noel did not want to use any facilities there.

If you have a disabled male with a female carer, should you go for the Gents or the Ladies? Personally I go for either, whichever is the more accessible. Apart from the occasional surprised look from a man at the urinals, no one ever raises any objections either way. In out of the way locations it might be necessary to find the nearest bush! Travelling by car, the call of nature can always be satisfied by the appropriate bottle.

We have hired cars on several occasions, especially on our short trips to England. Most cars will accommodate a wheelchair in the boot. Scooter owners would obviously have to check the size more carefully.

Every individual is different, and this is equally true of people with disabilities and their carers. What works for one person may not be possible for others. We have found what works for us.

We hope you have enjoyed sharing our experiences and if you are in a similar position, we hope our comments have been helpful and may make you want to visit some of the places yourselves.

Noel is 82 and I am 75. We intend to keep traveling for as long as we are able. The years since his stroke have thrown up different problems. Initially he could walk a very short distance with a walking stick if I held his arm. With considerable assistance he could get in a coach. That became steadily more difficult and is now, I suspect, impossible as he can no longer balance well enough to walk. Add to that the deterioration of his one arthritic hand...

But we don't intend to give up. Life exists to be enjoyed. There is a lot of world out there waiting to be explored and we will adapt to get there... We have Russia in our sights for 2010.